# RUN FARTHER, RUN FASTER

# RUN FARTHER, RUN FASTER

BY JOE HENDERSON

WORLD

World Publications, Inc.
Mountain View, California

**Recommended Reading:**

*Runner's World* magazine, Box 366,
Mountain View, CA 94042; $13.00/year
Write for a free catalog of publications.

**Library of Congress Cataloging in Publication Data**

Henderson, Joe, 1943 -
   Run farther, run faster

   1. Running. I. Title
GV1061.H39          796.4'26          78-64507
ISBN 0-89037-162-8

World Publications
Mountain View, CA

To Dean Roe, Walt Stanton, Chris Salberg, and Bob Karnes—
the coaches who taught me to race. And to Bert Nelson and
Bob Anderson—the publishers who let me say, "Don't take it
too seriously."

# Table of Contents

**Other Works by the Author**

*Long Slow Distance* (1969)
*Road Racers and Their Training* (1970)
*Thoughts on the Run* (1970)
*Run Gently, Run Long* (1974)
*Long Run Solution* (1976)
*Jog, Run, Race* (1977)

I've been up and down this highway
far as my eyes can see.
No matter how fast I run
I can never seem to get away from me.
No matter where I am
I can't help thinking
I'm just a day away
from where I want to be.*

*Jackson Browne*

# Foreword

A revolutionary is where you find him. He needn't come from Watts or Haight-Ashbury, Cuba or Algeria, or even thirteenth-century Italy. He could be the guy next door. He needn't be named Abbie Hoffman, Che Guevara, or even Thomas Aquinas. He could be called Joe Henderson.

Joe Henderson looks like a typical guy next door. Thirty-five years old and out of Iowa, he has the smile and style of the heartlands of America. But he has fallen for that old Socratic saw that the unexamined life is not worth living. The first result was revolt, rebellion, and a booklet called *Long Slow Distance—The Humane Way to Train,* published ten years ago. A flood of other books, booklets, and articles have followed, whose common theme is to liberate the runner and turn his sport into a happy and enjoyable occupation.

The LSD method of running that Henderson espouses is not new. He has simply systematized it and, in effect, founded a new order, a new sect that has bid pain, suffering, and sacrifice good-bye.

Henderson has resurrected the ideas of one of the greatest long-distance runners of all time, Arthur Newton. (Henderson calls him "the father of LSD.") Newton, who ran in the 1920s, had only two rules:

1. You must train as frequently as possible.

2. You must never permit yourself to approach real exhaustion.

"Run," said this quiet master of the roads, "in an easy and serene manner."

The words of Newton have not influenced many of the experts in the coaching and training professions. Few, if any, subscribe to the iconoclastic theory that you can train easier, perhaps race faster (though Henderson tries to downplay this claim about LSD), and enjoy the process a lot more. It does seem too good to be true. The first commandment has always been, "To train is to endure pain." How can you be helped by this "aimless plodding," as some critics term LSD? Isn't this method dull, boring, time-consuming, and inefficient?

The LSD disciples say just the opposite. Far from being dull and boring, running has become, according to one convert, "the bright light of my day." Another of them says, "To run down the road at a leisurely pace, enjoying the rhythm of my own body, is truly the sport of kings."

Some runners race quite well after training with LSD. Most of them, however, say they would keep running the LSD way even without a racing payoff. Joe Henderson is a revolutionary not because his writings have produced a wave of faster runners, but because he has spawned happier ones.

—George Sheehan, M. D.

# Introduction

A beast lives in me. I manage to keep him hidden most of the time, but I've never completely tamed him. He still breaks loose now and then. The beast is the irrational side of me. It competes, it races against the clock, it hurries and worries, it ignores all the body's signs that read, "Slow down! Take it easy!" The beast does all the things the rational side of me says I shouldn't do.

I let him have his way. I let the beast think he's running wild for a little while because if I didn't, he might cause even more trouble by attacking his cage in frustration. But I always keep a loose leash on him so I can regain control before he hurts anyone.

Metaphors aside, what I do is race. I go all out at distances as short as a half-mile and as long as 26 miles. I race hard, because I know no other way to race than to rub against the jagged edge of exhaustion. This, of course, seems to contradict all the calm sensible things I said in my earlier books about gentle, long running. I neither deny the charge nor admit that what I have said is wrong.

Everyday running and occasional racing are different animals. Running is the rational one, like the tame family dog. Racing is the irrational one, like the wolf that domestication hasn't quite bred out of the pet.

About 95 percent of the time, my running is quite tame. But I know I still have a hidden wild streak; so I leave a little room for it to break free.

Racing serves many purposes. It is a chance to see friends, to work against the clock, to test myself against the distance and the elements. But mostly it is a place to run like crazy—to have the same feelings our earliest ancestors did when they ran for their lives and won. Racing puts back some of the thrill of risk-taking that a rational, safe life lacks.

I urge every runner to race. If you've read my books *Run Gently, Run Long* or *The Long Run Solution,* it may sound out of character for me to praise such hard work. It's like listening to Steve Martin trying to be serious. But I am serious. I recommend racing to everyone—as long as you keep the beast on a leash and can yank him back under control before he masters you.

I've been a racer longer than a runner. By that I mean that at first I trained only to race and didn't begin to run just to be running until much later. I raced hard for fifteen years, totaling 492 events at distances from 100 yards to 100 miles in those years. I raced on indoor and outdoor tracks, over the countryside, and on the roads. I dropped out of my first mile race, ran 5:51 in the next, and eventually improved by 90 seconds and won seven state high school titles. I raced on a major university team. Then I turned to marathoning, ran my first in 2:49, and have slowed by 30 minutes in the 30 races since then.

I don't race nearly as often or as fast as I used to, because I don't train and think as I did then. I run casually, but I still race ten or so times a year. I'm as happy with the results as when I went a minute per mile faster, because the beast has gotten the hard workouts he needs.

I say these things about myself for two reasons. First, I've never thought of myself as unique from other runners. If the beast lives in me, he must be in most of us. You must want the same chance to run wild that I do. Second, I have practical experience  to pass along. I'm qualified to teach, if only because I've spent so many races teaching myself. This book grew out  of the things I've learned about my own racing. My lessons won't suit you perfectly, but they'll help you avoid the time-wasting, painful mistakes I've made.

This is an elective course. I assume you're taking it voluntarily, and that this indicates a certain amount of faith in the teacher's knowledge. For my part, I assume you aren't a beginning runner but that you have taken the prerequisite classes in running theory. Therefore, I won't spend much time reviewing old material or quoting authorities to back up what I say. We have more important ways to fill these few hours together.

This book was mine as I lived the research and wrote the manuscript. Now, it's yours. I have drawn the skeleton of racing techniques. You now have to add the flesh and life to it. I told you how I learned to live with the beast in me. You now have to make peace with yours by adapting my hints to your needs. I gave you my start. You now have to finish it in your way.

*Joe Henderson*
*Pebble Beach, 1979*

# Part One:

# Preparing for It

# 1

# **What This Book Isn't**

For the eighth straight year, I did not race the Bay-to-Breakers in 1978 in nearby San Francisco. I felt like the only runner in the Bay Area who didn't, as 15,000 were there. My absence was more a comment on me than on the size and state of that event. I tell everyone to try it at least once, but I won't race it myself anymore. Three times is enough; I'm beyond the Bay-to-Breakers now. I'm happier taking a run by myself that morning than fighting the crowds in San Francisco. I now run to avoid crowds rather than increase their size by one.

The word *beyond* is important here. I use it in place of *above* so no one will think I think I'm better than the crowd that races. I'm not. I ran with the crowd at one stage of my running life when racing was important to me, and now I've dropped out. My evolution has taken me into the mass, through it, and out the other side.

*Evolution*. That's the word I need to explain how interests change. The "Henderson theory of evolution" tells what may happen to all of us. When I try to explain it in talks to running groups, heads start nodding—but not in agreement. My description of the "theory" gets so twisted it induces a sleep response. No one seems to understand what I'm saying or to see himself in it. I saw how they felt when I read an interview John Stewart did with me for the *Los Angeles Times*. I resist the urge to edit what I said there. I told him there are three levels of runners, each with a different main reason for doing it—joggers, racers, and fun-runners. I told him:

> Joggers are doing it primarily for the exercise. The racers are doing it primarily to win. But there is this big group in the middle who I would call fun-runners. Their main attachment to running is a form of recreation. They would probably continue to run even if all races were cancelled. I would definitely put myself in this group.
>
> The others, in a way, are dead-ends. Very few people can become good, high-level racers or can stay up there very long. At the other side of the coin, jogging is in a sense a dead-end because many of the rewards are so far away. There has to be a stronger attachment than simply the somewhat negative emphasis on not dying.

My message there seems to be:

1. Runners forever belong in one of the three pigeonholes.
2. Only one of those holes is worth anything; running for fitness and competition are a waste of time.
3. I run the one true path to happiness.

But none of these is true. If I thought they were, I would be denying my own history and the way I evolved as a runner. I have run for different reasons at different times, and none was any less important or less exciting than the others when I was there.

I'll define the stages as quickly and clearly as I can. They form the basis of the "theory of evolution" that gives this book a theme and a focus. Though I see three stages, I don't use the terms jogger, racer, and runner for them. That implies too sharp a division between one stage and the next. We never completely leave one level behind as we move to a new one; we just modify the old in adopting the new. The evolutionary lines are blurred; the changes come gradually.

My evolution was as follows. First, I ran for exercise. I ran alone or with a few friends who were similarly unfit. Running was new to me, and I did it clumsily.

Next, I ran for competition. Once I knew I could finish my runs, I wanted to run them faster. I verified this by the watch, by my place beside the other runners in the race, and by the reactions of the crowd. I ran to race, and I raced in bigger and bigger events.

Finally, I ran for running itself. I tired of the chase, the crowds, and the stresses of racing. I ran alone again or with a few friends, but I wasn't stumbling anymore; I knew exactly where I was going. I got exercise, but only as a by-product. I ran some races, but I no longer looked at them as all-important. Since I've never thought of myself as one-of-a-kind, I assume other runners go through a similar evolution.

**Stage one: struggle to get into shape.** The length of stage one depends on how long you have spent getting out of shape. It takes about one month for each year of inactivity. If you're in your thirties and haven't run since junior high, you may struggle for two years before overcoming the decay and starting to look for a new challenge.

**Stage two: competence leads to competition.** Stage two begins close to home, usually with solo races against the watch. Then come races among your team if you are on one. Then, come dual meets for school runners and fun-runs for older ones. As your racing improves, your speed and the distance you run grow. You train harder. You get serious and stay that way for perhaps five years. That's about all any runner can handle before he tires of the strain and the sacrifice, or is broken down by it. After a few hard years, you're ready to slow down.

**Stage three: running for running's sake.** Stage three involves running as recreation, as a habit, for fun. You still stay in better shape than those who run just for exercise. You still can race as well as many people who train just to race. But those aren't your main reasons for running anymore. Stage three should be everyone's goal: to keep running without a promise of fitness, without the carrot of a race dangling on a stick in front of you, without needing to see a finish line.

But no one reaches this stage quickly or easily. You need lesser goals to take you there. The first is the fitness that lets you run comfortably for miles. You reach that goal rather quickly and easily, and then need a new one. This comes with wanting to run farther and faster. The best place to do that is in races. Racing can carry you for a long time as you move toward stage three, where you no longer care how far or fast you move—only that you keep moving.

Race until you don't need races anymore. There have never

been more chances to do it. I'm not overstating by saying we've had a racing revolution in the 1970s. I remember when the only people who competed were skinny, fast men in their late teens and twenties, plus a few "old guys" in their thirties who didn't know when to quit. That wasn't more than ten years ago.

Now, runners who never thought of themselves as athletes make up most of the field in long-distance events. Racers are more varied in age, sex, and—above all—ability than they were before. No one feels out of place, because there is always someone of similar ability running alongside, or there is always somewhere to hide in the crowd.

Crowds at races like the Bay-to-Breakers in San Francisco and the Peach Tree in Atlanta have grown so much (to 10,000-plus) that they aren't really races anymore. They are mass baptisms into organized running. Longer, more serious, events like the Boston, Chicago, Honolulu, and New York marathons draw 5,000 or more runners each. Dozens of other races have four-figure fields.

The size of races is significant for two reasons. First, single races now attract more people than ran in *all the races in the country* a few years ago. Second, since a dwindling percentage of these runners could be winners in the old sense of the word, they rewrote the definition of *winner* to produce a new type of runner to fit it.

I talk more in chapter 2 about how you can tell a winner and be one. But first, I describe the new type of racer. The book is for and about him. He is at stage two-and-a-half on my evolutionary scale. He approaches racing differently from the stage two athlete, who races to beat other people and their records, but not quite like the stage three fun-runner, who is content just to take part and to finish. The serious athlete is very ambitious; the fun-runner has little competitive drive. The person I call the "fun-racer" falls between the two. He works to improve his performances, but cares little how they match up against other people's marks.

Is this your book? You tell me.

**Do you want to race to get fit faster?** If so, don't bother reading any further. Racing is a dangerous way to learn to run, and is such hard work that it eats away at fitness instead of building it. I cannot feel responsible for you if you abuse yourself this way.

**Do you want to coast through to the finish?** Put this book away. You don't need my advice on racing, because you aren't racing if you aren't going all out.

**Do you want to climb to the high levels of racing, stepping over other runners to get there?** You get no help from me. You need more serious training advice than I give and tactical tricks I don't choose to offer.

**Do you want to race the extremes of distance, either the short dashes or the ultramarathons?** Sorry. The sprints haven't yet joined the revolution, and have no tradition or opportunity in fun-racing. The ultras are just too demanding for a fun-racer to take seriously, though he can run them cautiously.

However, if you answer "no" to these questions, and to all of those on the checklist, you've come to the right place. This is your book if:

1. You want to go far and fast, yet balance immediate success with long-term health and enjoyment.
2. You race not to beat other runners but to work with them to beat your own records.
3. You enter events in the mile-to-marathon range to give yourself plenty of records to break.
4. You train modestly, not to see how much work you can stand but how little you can do and still race well.
5. You race partly to join the racing revolution of the 1970s, but mostly to carry along your own evolution toward stage three.

### Self-Test 1
### What Do You Want?

1. Does your running career add up to less than three months and 100 miles?

2. Do you average less than one-third of the proposed racing distance daily in training?

3. Do you only want to struggle to the finish, no matter how much it hurts or how slow you go?

4. Do you only want to "run through" races to make the distance without extending yourself?

5. Do you view as "fanatics" runners who try to break five-minutes for the mile, one hour for 10 miles and three hours for the marathon?

6. Do you, as a rule, train more than 70 miles a week or work out twice a day?

7. Do you race as part of a team that works together under a coach?

8. Do you look at races primarily as "me-against-them" competitions?

9. Do you hope to win, set records, or both at a state, regional, national, or international level?

10. Do you hope your running will earn you a college scholarship, expense-paid travel to races, or similar benefits?

Note: If you answer "yes" to any of these questions, either back up to a more basic book (I highly recommend *Jog, Run, Race!*), move to something more advanced (I don't know a good book telling you how to win and doubt that books can teach this), or quit reading and be happy you're already at stage three.

# 2

## You'll Be A Winner

Running is the perfect sport. But before I say why, I assure you this isn't another exaggerated testimonial to its physical, sexual, or psychic powers. It might help you in those ways, but I don't promise it here. I only praise running for what it is—a sport. There are safer ways to exercise than this, better ways to meditate, quicker ways to get high, truer ways to find religion, and easier ways to have fun. But there is no finer sport. It attracts people for no more mystical reason than that they like to be winners at something. Objective measures of time and distance give every runner a chance to win—a claim few sports can make and a principle no other sport applies so well.

Running has grown quickly in the 1970s, and will keep growing because it offers to make winners of us all. Previously we thought a contest could have only one winner, and that no matter how good we got someone else would always be better. Therefore, we were all losers.

Now, distance running races tell us the opposite: *An event can have as many winners as it has runners. No one has to beat anyone else to win, but one must only deal well with the distance, the elements, his own time standards, and his own reluctant flesh and spirit.* This doesn't imply that you automatically win every time you race. If it were that easy, victory wouldn't mean much. But there is always the *chance* of winning, the hope of it. There is always a prize you can reach if you run up to your ability. This means a runner who crosses the finish line first might still lose in terms of his expectations; and

9

one who finishes a half-hour and a thousand places later might win by his. This possibility makes running the perfect sport for anyone who is tired of getting only life's booby prizes.

"The loser now will be later to win," wails Bob Dylan in "The Times They Are a'Changin'." He sings often to life's losers, and his words are popular and lasting because there are so many of us who sometimes lose.

Dylan probably hasn't run more in his life than the 10 steps from the stage door to his limousine to escape crazed fans. But he speaks better for me than any running writer I know. Maybe that's because I also spend many of my words giving aid and comfort to apparent losers. (I stress the world *apparent.*) I, too, am on the side of life's tortoises, because I am one. We are the slow ones, and we may not later be fast—but at least we'll be here after many fast-starting hares have dropped out.

But the big victories aren't ever permanent. The saddest people I know are those who've won prizes and acclaim for a few moments, lost them, then spend the rest of their days trying to relive those moments.

For both the tortoises and hares, then, I list what I sense are the new definitions of winning and losing. Few of these definitions have any resemblance to the ones I heard in the locker rooms of the fifties and sixties.

1.  Winning is realizing you have already won something by being in the running. You may not finish ahead of many other runners, but you have beaten the mass of people who choose to move on wheels instead of on foot.

    Losing is not starting, but being content to talk about what might be or might have been if . . .

2.  Winning is finishing the distance you set for yourself, however humble it might be. Speed is a gift your parents either gave you or couldn't. You had little to say about it, so the time you take to run your distance doesn't say much about your spirit. But endurance and persistence are largely trained-in and learned. Finishing is a victory of strong spirit over weak flesh.

    Losing is dropping out for no other reason than a weak will. Quitting in the face of actual or potential injury is wisdom, but giving up because of moderate inconvenience or mild discomfort is defeat.

3. Winning is measuring yourself against your potential. It is, first, learning to take pride in your progress, no matter how small. Later, it is taking pleasure in more subtle measures of victory that have little to do with time and place.

   Losing is matching yourself against everyone else who runs. This is self-defeating, because few people ever win this way, and those who do don't keep it up very long.

4. Winning is counting the number of runners ahead of you and recognizing your relative ability. You look up to them for advice and inspiration without viewing them with feelings of envy or inferiority.

   Losing is being intimidated out of the sport by those ahead of you or counting as inferior anyone who comes in later.

5. Winning is working with other runners so all of your results are better than any of you could have achieved alone. It is in one sense selfish; you use someone to raise yourself. But it is constructive competition in the sense that it can lift everyone.

   Losing is cutting someone else down so you can look taller. It is interfering in any way, physically or psychologically, with another runner's progress.

6. Winning is accepting results as they come, knowing that an occasional bad run will come even to those of us who look at competition this way. Bad runs are important as contrasts to help you appreciate the good ones.

   Losing is choosing to ignore the real results and to quote exaggerated ones instead. It is calling a 9½-mile course "about 10 miles," or calling a time of 59:59 "in the mid-50s."

7. Winning is learning from your bad experiences. Such experiences often teach more than the good ones because they force you to look for relief. I'm not saying you should intentionally make mistakes so you can learn from them; enough will happen automatically. But turn a minus into a plus when it opens.

Losing is refusing to accept failure as a teacher or neglecting to examine the reasons for failing.

8. Winning is standing on the shoulders of the giants. It is absorbing the written and spoken lessons of people who've run before, instead of using up an entire career resolving by trial and error the puzzles that already have been solved.

Losing is refusing to share with others your solutions to running puzzles or claiming someone else's solutions as your own.

9. Winning is continuing to run after fate has decided that you are past your prime and will never again break a personal record. It is continuing when there are no races left to run.

Losing is setting goals you either can't reach or can touch too easily. Goals are stopping places if they're made too rigid and important. If you don't reach them, you stop from frustration; if you reach them too quickly, you stop with no other peaks left to climb.

10. Winning is knowing you are only as good as your last run. The good effects and feelings don't store well, so you have to renew them all the time. Mediocre fresh runs are far better than spectacular stale ones.

Losing is living in the past. It is trying to restore old glories to the condition they were in during their short life.

### Self-Test 2
### What Have You Done?

1. Do you ever imagine yourself to be a sports hero?

2. Have you envied the talented athletes you watch or read about, and wished you could join them?

3. Do you generally think of yourself as a "loser" in sports talent?

4. Were you ever the last kid chosen for a schoolyard team?

5. Were you ever told not to bother trying a sport because "you aren't good enough"?

6. Were you ever cut from a team?

7. Did it bother you to work as hard as anyone on a team, and then watch someone else get all the glory?

8. Are you reluctant now to enter a sports event, fearing failure or "looking bad"?

9. Are you hungry enough for victory that you'll accept it under the terms I define in this chapter?

10. Are you ready to make *yourself* your sports hero?

Note: The more "yes" answers you give, the more ready you are for this book.

# 3

# A Few Words on Training

John Steinbeck, the author whose work I read with the greatest awe and envy, taught me this. He said he wasn't ready to write a book until he could tell what it was all about in a sentence. It sometimes took him years to reduce thousands of words into that simple a message.

This is my first book that concentrates purely on racing. I waited to write advice on races and preparing for them until I could say it all in 10 words or less. Of course, I fill the book with 50,000 other words, but they only amplify the basic few. The words look so simple here, as boldfaced subheads dividing a short chapter into just eight parts. But each word marks the successful end to a long trail of mistakes. You can read in a few minutes things I didn't stumble onto for many years. Ironically, by the time I found what the words were and how to apply them, I was too far along as a racer to use the lessons.

But I didn't mind making mistakes or taking so long to correct them. It wasn't wasted motion. While I hurt myself too badly to race well once I'd learned how, I wrote enough warnings to steer other runners onto clearer, safer courses.

I suffered for you. I don't want to sound like a martyr, because I'm as selfish as the next runner. I kept experimenting only to save myself. But in the end, I was like the canary sent down into the mine shaft to sniff out danger, to sacrifice himself if necessary so others could proceed more safely. Remember as you read these words how far I went down into the pits to test them.

## 1. Gentle

I can't tell you in numbers what your "gentle" pace is, because I don't know what my own is. It can't be stated in minutes per mile. My time changes from month to month with up and down swings in my condition. It's different on long and short runs, when I'm alone or in a crowd, when I'm inspired or depressed. It even shifts wildly from mile to mile within individual runs as I warm up and tire, or go up hills and down. But the effort never changes much. It's almost always gentle.

Gentle is a feeling in the bones, a state of mind. It's a feeling that running is too good to hurt all the time, an attitude that it goes best when it is relaxed. The easiest way to run gently is to run *with* time instead of *against* it. Fill a period of time; don't try to run a distance in shorter and shorter times. An hour is an hour, no matter how fast or slowly it's run. When running by time, the tendency is to go gently, not hard. By making friends with the watch, you tend to make friends with yourself. That's essential to long-term running.

## 2. Long

Running "long" has two meanings—one daily and the other stretching far into the future. Both should give an outlook that leaves no room for a sense of hurry or worry. The first involves setting aside a block of time each day as mine alone. I have my hour or so—my "holy hour" I call it. I guard it jealously and allow no intrusions. I fill much of this time with gentle running, but I leave enough air on both sides so I never feel I'm rushing to get to or get away from it.

The first half-hour of the run makes me fit. But the second half-hour makes running worth doing. So, the first part of the run is the warm-up, and few runners find it either easy or fun. I know I never do. These are the preliminaries I have to endure to get to the good part where my legs flow as if they have a mind of their own, and my mind is free to think of things beyond where the next step goes down. The second half-hour makes me want to keep coming back for more.

The other part of "long" is the view that there is no finish line in my running. I have no urge to get things done in a hurry, because I have lots of tomorrows. As the days add up, my running has a growing sense of consistency and continuity.

## 3. Steady

A runner adapts slowly to his work. He has to sneak up on bigger loads by taking many small, quiet steps instead of making explosive leaps at them. But the little gains add up to more in the long run than do the sporadic lunges. It's the old tortoise-and-hare principle of "steady pace wins the race." It's a matter of consistency.

One day doesn't amount to much. Any reasonably fit twelve-year-old with no running experience could do the 45 minutes or so that I average each day. But I don't count my running by minutes per day. I look at it with a longer view—over months and years. In a month's time, my rather puny daily total adds up to a full day of running. In a year, I spend almost two weeks on the run. My deep well of fitness doesn't come, then, from great floods of effort, but from quietly adding a few drops every day. I sometimes have to miss a day, but I never plan any days off, nor do I like missing them. After you've been running a few years, it gets harder *not* to run than to keep doing it.

## 4. Loose

The hardest of the lessons for me to learn was running loose—that is, to run from my guts and not from my head. The head wants to stick strictly to a preset routine, even when voices farther down in me say otherwise. This happens because the need for staying loose conflicts somewhat with the urge to run steadily.

To resolve the conflict, I say: Realize that work and recovery are equal parts of the running puzzle, and that no one can run hard or long every day. At best, you feel strong—and have the chance to go hard and long—a time or two a week. Hope for three, figure on two, and realistically expect one of these days each week. Don't try to force them when they aren't there. Simply start, then stay loose enough to go longer or to stop short, as your feelings dictate.

## 5. Cycles

Most runners can't recover overnight. They need 48 hours to throw off the effects of even a mildly long or hard run, and 72 hours or more to get over a racelike effort. They don't need to stop cold to recover, but they must not push themselves when tired or sore.

I balance the two apparently conflicting principles of "steady" and "loose" by being consistently inconsistent. I run in regular cycles that swing from harder to easier and back again. I've learned to identify pretty closely my own work/recovery cycle, and to cooperate with it.

My normal cycle is three days—one day of long running and the next two short. In my case "long" is 1½ to 2 hours on the roads. "Short" is 30 to 45 minutes, usually on grass or dirt. I run through two of these cycles a week. (The Biblical tradition of a day of rest each week has a physical basis. We probably need that day off, but I almost never take it. Instead, I run easier yet on the week's leftover day—usually Sunday.)

There are long, seasonal cycles, too. As an ex-farmer, I know you can't plant, grow, and harvest continually in the same soil. Somewhere in the cycle, the land needs a break—and so does the farmer.

I've found that I have natural six-month cycles. Each has two highs and two lows of about three months each, more or less paralleling the seasons of the year. I'm high at spring planting time and again at fall harvesting, low in the cold of winter and the heat of summer. I either choose to run less in summer and winter than in spring and fall—or nature chooses it for me with a series of injuries and illnesses.

## 6. Stop

Stop and walk in midrun. Take time out to catch your breath, to loosen up, to enjoy a nice view, or to water the bushes. I've learned rather late in my running life that there's no better way to make the long distances seem shorter and to make bad days more tolerable.

I seldom go more than a half-hour at a time now without taking a five-minute break. It's a form of interval training, which has as its basis the principle that the way to go longer and easier is to divide the work into smaller blocks. It works.

## 7. Speed

Make the running easier by doing some of it hard. This seems even more contradictory than the last statement (that the way to go longer is to go shorter), but I've found it to be at least as true. Much as I love gentle running, it puts the legs into a rut of short, tight, low strides. I grow stiff from hours of this. Speeding up and stretching out for a minute or so, recovering, and then repeating it another time or two puts life back into tired legs. When they have this bounce, they're less likely to get hurt.

I do one fast minute for each gentle 20, or 5 percent of the total. I do it more for the immediate effects on my legs than for future racing benefits.

## 8. Race

Training builds up, racing tears down. Before you race, then, be sure you've built up enough so you can stand the tearing down. That means averaging at least one-third of the longest racing distance each day for many weeks to be sure you can go far enough, as well as doing short runs at the speed of the shortest race so you know you can go fast enough. Put distance and speed together in the race.

After racing, take enough time to repair the damage done. Allow two days of recovery for each mile of the race—one easy day to clear away debris left by the race, and the other to build training back to the old level and higher. Build more between races than you break down during them.

### Self-Test 3
### What Do You Do Wrong?

1.  Do you measure all your runs and time them precisely, trying to improve your record each day?

    Do you find it hard to finish runs and to think immediately of running again the following day?

2.  Does your running often seem boring and seldom give the good feelings you'd been promised?

    Do most runs last less than 30 minutes?

3.  Do you typically run fewer than five days a week?

    Do you typically run in bursts of effort and enthusiasm, broken by many days or weeks off?

4. Do you try to run the same distance at the same effort every time out and expect the same results?

   Are you reluctant to change from a scheduled run even when you feel extra-bad or extra-good?

5. Do you expect to recover fully within 24 hours after hard runs and wonder what is wrong when you don't?

   Do you think something is wrong when you can't run the same pace and mileage in summer and winter that you run in spring and fall?

6. Do you feel you're cheating if you stop and walk during a run?

   Do you find it too hard to extend your distances much beyond the length of your average ones?

7. Are you a "shuffler" who has a hard time speeding up or striding out?

   Are your legs chronically tight and heavy, or do they carry low-grade soreness much of the time?

8. Do you want to race, but find a faster pace too painful to maintain?

   Do you want to race, but find a longer distance too exhausting to finish?

Note: If you answer "yes" to any of these questions, check the word with the corresponding number—"1. Gentle," "2. Long," etc.—for possible solutions.

# 4

# **Read Before You Race**

Racing is glamorous only when dreaming about it and planning for it before you run, and when recalling it and bragging about it after you finish. The racing itself holds little romance. What it mostly does is hurt. The amount it hurts depends on the odds you give yourself. If you take on a race you're ready for, the pain is tolerable and brief. But if you wade in blindly, fighting with more guts than sense, you get beat up and stay that way for some time.

Mild pain is part of racing, maybe even a key reason to race. You see how well you can work against it. But inflicting severe, lasting damage is not the point. You try to avoid that.

You aren't ready to race, then, until you can accept mild pain. And you aren't ready until you immunize yourself against injury. Endurance training is the only known vaccine against these stresses of racing. The better you train, the more small hurts you can handle and the fewer big ones you contract. (Of course, you might overdose on training and hurt yourself that way, too. But I assume here that you train wisely.)

No one is protected against the blows of distance racing until he has taken at least 30-minute training shots daily for a couple of months. I don't condone racing on less than that amount of basic work. Until you reach the half-hour level, you have bigger concerns: getting into shape and learning to enjoy running.

If you're now doing less running, delay your racing plans. First, build up the reserves to handle the normal pains and hold off the abnormal ones. Run gently and long, for as many weeks as you need to reach a half-hour of steady, comfortable running. To show you how you might do this, I've adapted a three-month basic running plan from *Jog, Run, Race.* Determine the amount of running you do now. Start with the next week and move up steadily from there to the end of the schedule. This much running will get you ready to *finish* races of 1-10 miles. But to go longer or faster, or to put the two together, you'll need to train.

Technically speaking, running and training are not the same. All training involves running, but all running isn't training. The difference in the two is more than word-play. While you run for its benefits as you're doing it and right afterward, training is preparation for what it might produce later. Running is an end in itself, while training is a means to an end.

There are more differences between running and training:

- Training is more focused, pointed at a single day in the near future, and at a place, time, and distance when the training yields the best possible result.

- Training is more carefully planned, both so it is timed to give the result you want when you want it, and to avoid mistakes that would lay all the preparation to waste.

- Training is harder, because racing is hard work. You must prepare both your body and mind to accept the extra effort instead of rebelling when facing it for the first time.

- Training sometimes hurts because, as I've said, racing hurts. You can no more escape the pain than a swimmer can keep from getting wet. Take the plunge into discomfort in training so it doesn't take you by surprise in the race.

The whole idea of training might be to eliminate the bad surprises from the race. Although we never completely succeed, we probably wouldn't want to. If racing was too safe it wouldn't carry the thrill it does. Training isn't intended to eliminate all risks. It simply brings the odds on success or failure down to an even-money bet.

I won't bog you down here with a lot of training theory. The guiding principles are enough to know:

- Training comes in two parts—"base work" and "sharpening." It is likely you have already laid your base without even thinking of it as training. You have done this via everyday distance running, which lets you go long, comfortably. Sharpening, or "peaking," involves learning to go harder and faster. This is simulating or rehearsing the race to get used to some of its stresses.

• Race rehearsals involve (1) running far enough to be able to handle the race's distance, (2) running fast enough to handle its pace, and (3) simulating the setting of the event by running at a similar time of day and on a similar surface and terrain.

• Prepare to run the distance of your longest race and the speed of your shortest. Say you want to race in the 1-to 10-mile range. Train to handle the distance of the 10 and the speed of the one.

Here are the requirements and rehearsals for races of five different types: fun-runs, short distances (two miles and less), medium distances (3-10 miles), long distances (10 miles to marathon), and ultra-long (beyond the marathon).

## Fun-Runs

The least traumatic way to break into racing is on the most informal level. Take one small step up from your everyday running by joining other low-level racers for a fun-run. Start with a rather short distance, similar to what you do in daily running at a slower pace. For most beginners, five miles is far enough.

*Requirements:* Ability to run the full distance comfortably in practice before attempting it for time. Familiarity with the maximum speed required in the race.

## Two Miles and Less

These are speed races, usually run on the track. For anyone considering running them seriously, the distance is no problem; the difficulty comes in maintaining high speed. Get used to running fast but in control, so you're able to spread your effort over the full distance. Practice pace work, whenever possible at the same place you'll be racing (for instance, the track).

*Requirements:* Fun-runs at similar distances. Have a personal record you're trying to break.

**Three to Ten Miles**

I refer to these as "middle distances," because they require some of the speed of the mile and some of the endurance of the marathon. In training, pay attention to both fast and long work. The races can be held anywhere—track, cross-country, or road—so practice at the appropriate place. Give special emphasis to hills if you expect there to be any on the race course. Hill running is a learned skill.

*Requirements:* Experience in races at distances near the bottom of this range. Practice runs at the top of the range or longer. Average at least 3-5 miles a day in training.

**Ten Miles to Marathon**

Beginners shouldn't worry about speed in the long road races. Distances come first, and it's enough of a chore just to finish these races now without thinking about how fast you are. Train to survive the first race. If you're racing in this distance range, it's inevitable that you'll try a marathon soon, so the training recommendations here center on the 26-miler.

*Requirements:* Successful completion of "middle-distance" (3-to-10-mile) races. Training at least 60 miles a week for 6-8 weeks before the race, with regular long runs of at least 18 miles.

**Beyond the Marathon**

Beginning ultramarathoners are usually veteran racers. They have to be experienced even to consider running anything longer than 26 miles. The next logical step is 50 kilometers, which is five miles farther than the marathon, but ultramarathoning truly begins at 50 miles.

*Requirements:* At least one full marathon and preferably several. Training at least 60 miles a week for eight weeks before the race, with regular long runs of 20 miles and more.

But I'm sprinting far ahead of myself by talking about races this fast and long. First, I must say more about training. Your capacity to absorb the blows of a race is decided there, long before you get to the starting line.

# Table 1
## Basic Training

**WEEK ONE**

| Day | Suggested | Actual |
|---|---|---|
| 1 | 10 minutes | _____ |
| 2 | 20 minutes | _____ |
| 3 | 15 minutes | _____ |
| 4 | 20 minutes | _____ |
| 5 | 10 minutes | _____ |
| 6 | 30 minutes | _____ |
| 7 | Optional | _____ |
| Total | 105 minutes | _____ |
| Average | 15 minutes | _____ |

**WEEK TWO**

| Day | Suggested | Actual |
|---|---|---|
| 1 | 15 minutes | _____ |
| 2 | 20 minutes | _____ |
| 3 | 15 minutes | _____ |
| 4 | 20 minutes | _____ |
| 5 | 15 minutes | _____ |
| 6 | 35 minutes | _____ |
| 7 | Optional | _____ |
| Total | 120 minutes | _____ |
| Average | 17 minutes | _____ |

**WEEK THREE**

| Day | Suggested | Actual |
|---|---|---|
| 1 | 15 minutes | _____ |
| 2 | 25 minutes | _____ |
| 3 | 20 minutes | _____ |
| 4 | 25 minutes | _____ |
| 5 | 15 minutes | _____ |
| 6 | 35 minutes | _____ |
| 7 | Optional | _____ |
| Total | 135 minutes | _____ |
| Average | 19 minutes | _____ |

**WEEK FOUR**

| Day | Suggested | Actual |
|---|---|---|
| 1 | 15 minutes | _____ |
| 2 | 25 minutes | _____ |
| 3 | 20 minutes | _____ |
| 4 | 25 minutes | _____ |
| 5 | 20 minutes | _____ |
| 6 | 40 minutes | _____ |
| 7 | Optional | _____ |
| Total | 145 minutes | _____ |
| Average | 21 minutes | _____ |

**WEEK FIVE**

| Day | Suggested | Actual |
|---|---|---|
| 1 | 15 minutes | _____ |
| 2 | 30 minutes | _____ |
| 3 | 20 minutes | _____ |
| 4 | 30 minutes | _____ |
| 5 | 20 minutes | _____ |
| 6 | 45 minutes | _____ |
| 7 | Optional | _____ |
| Total | 160 minutes | _____ |
| Average | 23 minutes | _____ |

**WEEK SIX**

| Day | Suggested | Actual |
|---|---|---|
| 1 | 20 minutes | _____ |
| 2 | 30 minutes | _____ |
| 3 | 20 minutes | _____ |
| 4 | 35 minutes | _____ |
| 5 | 20 minutes | _____ |
| 6 | 50 minutes | _____ |
| 7 | Optional | _____ |
| Total | 175 minutes | _____ |
| Average | 25 minutes | _____ |

**WEEK SEVEN**

| Day | Suggested | Actual |
|---|---|---|
| 1 | 20 minutes | _____ |

**WEEK EIGHT**

| Day | Suggested | Actual |
|---|---|---|
| 1 | 20 minutes | _____ |

## WEEK SEVEN (cont.)

| | | |
|---|---|---|
| 2 | 35 minutes | _____ |
| 3 | 25 minutes | _____ |
| 4 | 35 minutes | _____ |
| 5 | 20 minutes | _____ |
| 6 | 55 minutes | _____ |
| 7 | Optional | _____ |
| Total | 190 minutes | _____ |
| Average | 27 minutes | _____ |

## WEEK EIGHT (cont.)

| | | |
|---|---|---|
| 2 | 40 minutes | _____ |
| 3 | 30 minutes | _____ |
| 4 | 40 minutes | _____ |
| 5 | 20 minutes | _____ |
| 6 | 1 hour | _____ |
| 7 | Optional | _____ |
| Total | 210 minutes | _____ |
| Average | 30 minutes | _____ |

## WEEK NINE

| Day | Suggested | Actual |
|---|---|---|
| 1 | 20 minutes | _____ |
| 2 | 40 minutes | _____ |
| 3 | 30 minutes | _____ |
| 4 | 40 minutes | _____ |
| 5 | 20 minutes | _____ |
| 6 | 1 hour | _____ |
| 7 | Optional | _____ |
| Total | 210 minutes | _____ |
| Average | 30 minutes | _____ |

## WEEK TEN

| Day | Suggested | Actual |
|---|---|---|
| 1 | 20 minutes | _____ |
| 2 | 40 minutes | _____ |
| 3 | 30 minutes | _____ |
| 4 | 40 minutes | _____ |
| 5 | 20 minutes | _____ |
| 6 | 1 hour | _____ |
| 7 | Optional | _____ |
| Total | 210 minutes | _____ |
| Average | 30 minutes | _____ |

## WEEK ELEVEN

| Day | Suggested | Actual |
|---|---|---|
| 1 | 20 minutes | _____ |
| 2 | 40 minutes | _____ |
| 3 | 30 minutes | _____ |
| 4 | 40 minutes | _____ |
| 5 | 20 minutes | _____ |
| 6 | 1 hour | _____ |
| 7 | Optional | _____ |
| Total | 210 minutes | _____ |
| Average | 30 minutes | _____ |

## WEEK TWELVE

| Day | Suggested | Actual |
|---|---|---|
| 1 | 20 minutes | _____ |
| 2 | 40 minutes | _____ |
| 3 | 30 minutes | _____ |
| 4 | 40 minutes | _____ |
| 5 | 20 minutes | _____ |
| 6 | 1 hour | _____ |
| 7 | Optional | _____ |
| Total | 210 minutes | _____ |
| Average | 30 minutes | _____ |

## WEEK THIRTEEN

| Day | Suggested | Actual |
|---|---|---|
| 1 | 20 minutes | _____ |
| 2 | 40 minutes | _____ |
| 3 | 30 minutes | _____ |
| 4 | 40 minutes | _____ |
| 5 | 20 minutes | _____ |
| 6 | 1 hour | _____ |
| 7 | Optional | _____ |
| Total | 210 minutes | _____ |
| Average | 30 minutes | _____ |

**Using the Schedule**

1. The full three-month program allows for an eight-week buildup of running times, followed by six weeks of maintaining a 30-minute daily average with a weekly one-hour run.

2. Racing isn't recommended until you have averaged a half-hour a day for one to two months.

3. Do all running at a pace that allows you to breathe easily and to finish comfortably.

4. On scheduled runs lasting less than 30 minutes, add walking breaks to bring the total to at least a half-hour.

5. The buildup progresses by about 10 percent per week. Don't try to increase it faster than that.

6. The schedule calls for three days of longer running alternated with shorter runs. The seventh (optional) day can be for rest or making up time lost during the week.

7. Start one week beyond your current average, filling in the amounts you actually run. Base all averages on seven-day weeks (divide totals by seven), whether you run every day or not.

## Self-Test 4
### Where Are You Now?

1. What is your current weekly total of miles or minutes?

2. Is this a typical week for you?

3. If the normal total is much higher or lower, what is it?

4. What is your daily average in miles or minutes in a typical week? (Divide by seven even if you don't run every day.)

5. If you count miles, how long do you take to run the average distance?

6. Using the average time, where do you now stand on the schedule (week number)?

7.  What has been your longest run to date (in minutes)?

8.  Is this longest run similar in time to the one recommended in the schedule for your week?

9.  If the scheduled run is longer, are you confident you can jump quickly to that amount? (If not, make up the difference in other runs during the week until you adapt to longer running.)

10. Do you need the basic training schedule? (You don't if you already average 30 minutes or more per week and are capable of doing occasional one-hour runs.)


Note: If you answer "yes" to the last question, enter the schedule one week above your current level, and progress as indicated.

# 5

## One Plan Fits All

I've known since 1971, when I watched Frank Shorter turn green and rush away from a post marathon dinner to throw up, that running is a great equalizer. We all feel the same hurts and joys. There are things in running that make the gods of the sport more human and make the least of us more noble. We share certain experiences.

I never saw this more clearly than during the 1977 National Running Week activities at Palo Alto, California. The world's two best marathoners of the time, Jerome Drayton and Bill Rodgers, admitted they were more frightened by talking for three minutes than by racing for 2¼ hours. Best-selling author Erich Segal, who has ridden with the jet set, deferred to big-name athletes like Marty Liquori. U.S. Senator Alan Cranston, a sprinter himself, asked one of his running constituents for training advice. This made us feel closer to them.

We are more alike than different in the way we run, too. That message came from speaker after speaker during the week. There seem to be a few simple principles and philosophies that apply to all of us almost equally.

Too often, we assume because runners like Drayton and Liquori race so fast that they dropped in from another planet; they must be made from different fiber than we are. We're misled, too, by the numbers they talk: 100-mile-plus weeks, 32-mile runs, 20 interval quarter-miles at 60 seconds each. We seldom hear about them doing base-building and recovery running at a comfortable pace.

Drayton, the 1977 Boston Marathon winner, said about 90

percent of his running is done at a seven-minute mile pace (quite relaxed for a man who races at sub-five-minute pace). Only the remaining 10 percent is hard training and racing. Liquori, the American 5000-meter record-holder, said much the same. On average, about 90 percent of his running is at a gentle seven-minute rate.

They do almost exactly what I do and what I now advise fun-racers to do—plenty of steady running at a comfortable pace for endurance-building and recovery, and a small but very important percentage of speed training and racing. Of course, Drayton and Liquori run faster since they're able and do more because they must, but the recipe is the same. This recipe is hardly new.

"We stand on the shoulders of giants," said Dr. George Sheehan during National Running Week. And we often don't even know the giants who are supporting us. Arthur Lydiard practiced this combination of easy and hard training twenty years ago, and Ernst van Aaken used it eariler.

Long ago, van Aaken wrote that the top runners of the future would not train any differently than anyone else; they would just do more of it. From what I heard at the 1977 Running Week, the future is here. I spoke of this in my talk that week. Afterward, a young man said, "You picked up the idea that everybody's the same?"

I nodded.

"Well, I got just the opposite impression. To me, the speakers were saying everybody's different."

"I think we both may be right," I said. "The general principles are much the same. Certain physical laws control all of us. But the specific applications of them are as different as our thumbprints because everyone has his own special abilities and needs."

A simple recipe begins here and runs through the book. I told its ingredients with the "words" in chapter 3 and I gave the amounts of each with the "requirements" in chapter 4. I've said in this chapter why one plan is broad enough to hold milers and marathoners, beginning racers and front-runners. I can keep the recipe simple because the principles that make it work are so simple. And I keep it simple because any plan that can't be memorized in one reading is too complex, as is one that takes more than a few words to define.

A definition of my running takes only a sentence: I average a gently paced 45-60 minutes a day, including a few minutes of walking and a few minutes of fast running.

In short, I take the same basic run over and over again, only changing its length, pace, and setting. I ask you to do the same. Adjust the amount of running to match the race distance, and set a pace to suit your ability. But stay within the recipe.

To review:

1. Set aside at least an hour a day for yourself, and fit into it at least a half-hour of running. (I use time periods in all schedules. If you'd rather run by distances, be sure you run for the full amounts of time listed.)

2. Plan to run six days a week, but cut runs short or take days off without feeling guilty when circumstances demand it.

3. Allow one "optional" day each week, so there's room in the schedule for unexpected misses or a place to make up lost time.

4. Alternate long and short runs, and make one of the "long" ones extra-long or else run a race. A typical week's pattern: Monday—short; Tuesday—long; Wednesday—short; Thursday—long; Friday—short; Saturday—longest run or race; Sunday—optional.

5. Run 90 percent of the time at a gentle, unhurried pace that lets you finish with the feeling you could do more.

6. Take time out to walk if you need it to keep the runs comfortable, but don't count the break time in the total for the run.

7. Add about 5 percent speed (that's one minute in twenty) each day by accelerating to a pace that gets you slightly winded.

8. Race the remaining 5 percent of the time. Be sure you're averaging runs of at least one-third of the race time each day in training, and that you recover and rebuild with two training days for each mile of the race.

### Self-Test 5
### What Do You Need?

1. What is the longest distance you expect to race?

2. What is the total time you expect to run for that distance (in minutes)?

3. What should be your average daily training time (divide race time by three to find the minimum)?

4. What would be your total running time for a week to attain this average (multiply by seven)?

5. What would be the length of your "short" run (about two-thirds of the average time, or 10 percent of the week's total; multiply total by 0.1)?

6. What would be the "long" run (about 1 1/3 the average or 20 percent of the week's total; multiply the total by 0.2)?

7. What would be the "longest" run (about twice the average or 30 percent of the week's total; multiply the total by 0.3)?

8. What would be your weekly schedule (times may have to be adjusted slightly to get the proper total)?

    Day One (short)＿＿＿＿＿＿＿＿＿＿＿＿

    Day Two (long)＿＿＿＿＿＿＿＿＿＿＿＿＿

    Day Three (short)＿＿＿＿＿＿＿＿＿＿＿

    Day Four (long)＿＿＿＿＿＿＿＿＿＿＿＿

    Day Five (short)＿＿＿＿＿＿＿＿＿＿＿＿

    Day Six (longest)＿＿＿＿＿＿＿＿＿＿＿

    Day Seven (optional)＿＿＿＿＿＿＿＿＿

    Total Time＿＿＿＿＿＿＿＿＿＿＿＿＿＿＿

9. If you plan to increase the present amount of running, what is the average time you want to attain?

10. What is your ultimate weekly schedule (follow the same procedure as in questions 1-8 above)?

Day One (short)_____
Day Two (long)_____
Day Three (short)_____
Day Four (long)_____
Day Five (short)_____
Day Six (longest)_____
Day Seven (optional)_____
Total Time_____

11. What is a safe rate of progress (adding 10 percent per week to the average)?

12. How many weeks will it take you to reach the training goal at this rate of progress?

## Notes on Schedule-Planning

- Bring your average to 30 minutes a day before entering races. The basic schedule in chapter 4 tells how to get there.

- Thirty minutes daily is adequate for races of 1-10 miles. Train more if you plan to race farther.

- Add fast runs each day in the amount of one minute per twenty of gentle running and at the pace of the shortest race you plan to do.

- "Optional" days are for rest or making up lost time. If you prefer to run every day, add another "short" day by taking a few minutes away from other runs.

- Cut down the amount of running by as much as 50 percent the week before and the week after a race.

# 6

# A Place to Start

The longest step you'll ever take as a runner is the first one into running, and the next longest is the first one into racing. The size of these two steps trips up too many people. Men and women who might be helped the most by running never get out the door, and those who might like racing best never get to the starting line.

I wrote in the booklet *Step Up to Racing:* "Some non-racers feel the same about competing as non-runners do about exercising. They're self-conscious. They think everyone will stare at them or judge them. They're afraid of 'looking bad.' "

In some ways, stepping up to racing is even harder than starting to run. I don't mean physically harder; you know and accept that. The psychological step is the hard one. You can slip out to run under cover of darkness and never tell anyone. You can slip out of it the same way, and no one but you has to know you quit. In a race, there seems to be no place to hide. Everyone else racing and watching can see what you do—or don't do. It's the latter part that increases your fears. What if you can't finish? Or worse, what if you finish last, as the officials are packing up to go home? Will the other runners, who have already showered, laugh at your puny efforts?

Perhaps our greatest fear in a world where "cool" is king is that we'll look like a fool in others' eyes. Don't worry. You probably won't look foolish while racing. But even if you do, there will be enough people around you making fools of themselves, too, that no one will notice you. That's the nice thing about the boom in racing. It has crowded the events so much that no one has to feel odd or alone. You can find plenty of company as well as hide in the crowd.

Choose a first race by two standards. The first is distance, which we've talked about for the last three chapters. Race a distance you know you're ready to handle. That shouldn't be more than 10 miles. The races available to beginners will probably be in the 3- to 10-mile range, on the roads.

The second standard is the crowd—its size and makeup. The larger the field, the better place it is to start racing—for reasons I've given and more. Races usually grow from the middle on back. Elite racers always show up, but slower ones need more coaxing. Also, newer racers aren't yet plugged into the communications network. They only hear about the big, well-publicized events like San Francisco's Bay-to-Breakers.

Every city needs a race like the 7½-miler from San Francisco Bay to the Pacific. (Fortunately, many cities do have one. Atlanta, for instance, draws a field almost as large for its 10-kilometer Peach Tree race. I use the Bay-to-Breakers as an example because it is the biggest and I know it best.) Like the city on the San Andreas, this event has its faults. Years ago, it quit being a race in the usual sense and became a mass run-in. With 15,000 runners in it now, it is both less and more than a race.

Anyone who wants to race it fast ends up being angry with the officials and other runners. There are too few of the former and too many of the latter. The start makes finishing times and places meaningless. Hundreds of runners move down Howard Street, sometimes blocks ahead of the starting line, or else use parallel streets to avoid the mob. Those in the crowd never find room to stretch out and run hard. They simply go with the stream, which oozes across the city like spilled molasses. Purists might say this is a perversion of racing, since there is no real start. (Every year, a few front-runners sprint away several minutes early and everyone follows. No official is foolish enough to step out and call "false start.") And there is no real finish. (Only the first few hundred places are recorded, and those none too accurately. The other runners read from an overhead clock at the finish line—if they get to the line. The crush stops most of them before they get there.) And there is no real running in between.

Some runners get upset that people make a joke of running the Bay-to-Breakers. Dogs wear official numbers. Two men run the distance dressed in a horse costume; several wear tuxedos; another has his team name tattooed on his chest. In 1977, two runners dressed as doctors carried a stretcher with a gorilla suit on it. They shouted, "Make way for a runner in distress!" as they parted the crowd. That joke turned sour as a twenty-five-year-old runner collapsed in Golden Gate Park. He died before reaching a hospital. The Bay-to-Breakers is a media circus, so of course the media pumped all the details out of this tragedy.

However, the real news of the race was not that someone had died, but that the event came off with so little trouble. Only four runners—less than one-tenth of 1 percent of the field—required hospital treatment. This was in a run in which most participants hadn't trained enough, if at all, and in which simple tramplings should have accounted for more than four serious injuries.

Most runners in the Bay-to-Breakers are content to flow along with the current, without pushing themselves or each other, and without worrying about their starting or finishing places. For many, it is a graduation procession. It means stepping up from neighborhood jogging to organized (well, semi-organized) running. This is the first event most of them hear about. It is a goal luring them to do more running. It is an introduction to other races in the area.

Harry Cordellos, a blind runner from San Francisco, ran his first race here. He said, "In that run, all the myths I had believed about the limitations of blind people were trampled by a thousand feet at the start. This race opened a whole new world to me, which I wouldn't have found otherwise. It has done the same for countless others, and for this reason alone the Bay-to-Breakers should continue for 50 million years."

This is an event for the not-too-serious-or-talented runner who wants to be a small part of something very large. Even runners who do it for other reasons recognize this.

Paul Geis, the winner in 1977, said, "I think it's really exciting that so many people participate. That's the important thing to remember. Sure, you have a couple of people trying really hard. But the fact that there are so many people just taking part in this makes it something special."

For many runners, the Bay-to-Breakers is their start in racing. Ninety percent of them have never run a race before, and maybe half of them will never race anywhere else. But a fair number will move on from here to smaller and better events where they can improve their pace and distance.

Their problem then becomes what type of races to run and where to find them. The choices and sources are far more abundant than new racers might think. Formal racing starts at 50 yards and extends to 24-hour runs. These events break down into categories: sprints—50-660 yards (or their metric equivalents); short distances—880 yards to two miles; middle distances—3-10 miles; long distances—between 6 miles and the marathon; marathons—only races of 26 miles, 385 yards; and ultramarathons—longer than 26.22 miles. The distances are run on indoor and outdoor tracks, and on cross-country (natural surfaces) and road courses.

Your first interest should be in the middle-distance road and cross-country races, because they usually are open to everyone. Entry requirements are simple: (1) membership in the Amateur Athletic Union or Road Runner Club (you can probably join when you sign up for the race); (2) payment of an entry fee (normally less than five dollars); and (3) mailing the entry blank before the deadline.

Lists of upcoming races aren't hard to find once you know where to start looking. As you may already know, local newspapers aren't much help. However, national and regional running publications list most major, and some minor, events. Check *Runner's World, The Runner,* and *On the Run* for the bigger national races. Such magazines as *Yankee Runner* (New England), *Running Times* (East and South), *Runner's Gazette* (East), *Stride On* (Midwest), and *Nor-Cal Running Review* (California) publish extensive regional schedules.

Once you join the Amateur Athletic Union (AAU) or the Road Runner's Club (RRC), officials in your area will put race information in your hands. But the best source of all is the runners you meet and talk with as you begin to race. Ask them where to race next.

### Self-Test 6
### Are You Ready?

1. Does your training have you ready to go to the starting line? (Check the training requirements in chapters 4 and 5.)

2. Do you have prerace experience at running long and fast? (Before entering a "real" race, try an informal fun-run with a group. *Runner's World* lists several hundred fun-run sites each month.)

3. Was the fun-run five miles (30 minutes) or less? (The race rehearsal shouldn't be longer than this distance or time. Otherwise, it might tire you out too much before the real thing.)

4. Is the first race you're entering a mass-participation race, open to all? (It should be, so you'll be sure to have plenty of company at your pace.)

5. Is the race 10 miles (60 minutes) or less? (Your training probably hasn't prepared you to go longer than this the first time.)

6. If the race is a metric distance, do you know what the distance is in miles? (Most events now are run in kilometers. The Appendix includes a chart for translating these distances to miles.)

7. Do you have the proper AAU or RRC credentials? (You must be a member of one organization or the other to enter most races. Their addresses are given in the Appendix.)

8. Have you filled out your entry blank, paid the fee, and mailed these on time? (Most races require you to enter before a deadline.)

9. Are you on anyone's mailing list for race information? (Local clubs, AAU districts, and RRC affiliates all supply this to their members. Important addresses are in the back of the book.)

10. Do you read one or more of the magazines listing race schedules? (See the Appendix for addresses of the major national and regional publications.)

Note: You should answer "yes" to all the above questions before racing. If you say "no" to any of them, take the corrective steps indicated.

# Part Two:

# Doing It

# 7

# The Last Days

Races are won or lost by the mistakes you make or avoid making. If I listed the mistakes that make runners lose, the results might surprise you. The smallest number would come during the event; most would happen in the days and weeks before the race. That's because race results aren't usually decided on race day. They are settled in the training period by the kind of foundation work you lay down. Training effects are slow in coming. They add up slowly, and they return slowly to help you in races. That means you don't feel stronger today from the training you did yesterday. Instead, you use what you did last week, last month, even last year. The good reactions are delayed that much.

The point is this: you can't cram the last week with all the training you can stand and expect to make up for the work you didn't do earlier. It's too late to win this way, but you still have time to beat yourself in the last few days.

This chapter gives a lesson on surviving the week before a race. Heavy training is over for this one. Nothing you do will help, though it still can hurt. This is a time for waiting, resting, planning, but most of all for not making mistakes.

What I'm about to say may sound so obvious that you wonder why I bothered writing it or why you bother reading it. Maybe it is just common sense. But I know the first thing to leave me in the last week before I raced seriously was my good sense. I made my dumbest moves at times when I could least afford them. I tried to do training I couldn't use and forgot to do things I needed.

So the section that follows includes a set of do's and don'ts for the last week. Use it during this awkward period between the end of hard training and the start of hard racing, a time when you may blow the chance to use the training as well as you're able.

### 1. Do Let Your Training Slip

When I was in college, the team made a southern trip each spring. One week we travelled so much I could only do token training. I ended the week with a 4:18 mile—my best.

I said, "If I can run that fast without training, think what I can do next week if I work at it."

On Monday I ran three half-miles in 2:05, 2:03, and 2:01.

"I'm ready for a 4:10 mile this week," I thought.

Tuesday I tore a calf muscle while trying to work hard again. I didn't run at all that Saturday and didn't run well the rest of the season. This taught me the lesson I pass on now. Let yourself be lazy. Short, easy training is the only kind that can help you this late. The only thing that might help more would be total rest, but few runners will let themselves take that. So the little running you do in the last week is for the mind. It keeps you from thinking you've lost everything.

Take the last long, hard run a full week before the race. Follow that run with whatever you usually do on the optional day. If it's rest, great; enjoy it. Then coast through the last week. Perhaps take off the next-to-last day before the race to insure you're fresh. Take a loosening-up run the last day, as much to shake out the nerves as to stretch the muscles. The key rule with last-week training, as with any radical experiments at this time, is: when in doubt, don't!

### 2. Do Plan Your Moves

It's a common failing to dream about ends when we should be concentrating on means. In running terms, this means we're tempted to think too much about how we'll look and feel as we rush across the finish line, and too little about the hidden miles we slog through to get there. Yet, as I've said, races aren't won at the finish line, but in the long miles leading up to it. This is true of the time put into training, where a hundred miles underlie each racing mile. And it's true in the time spent planning moves that appear spontaneous on race day.

The time to think through the details is now, before the race starts. Be realistic and a little bit cautious. Base your plans on what you have done in training and what you *think* (not hope) you can do in the race. Anticipate problems and solve them before they surprise you too late.

What is your time goal? What kind of pace will you need at the checkpoints to get it? What effects might the weather and terrain have on your plans? What should you wear? What should you do for a warmup? Where should you stand at the start? Who, if anyone, should you follow as a pacer? What, if anything, should you drink?

Think about these. Plan the right answers to these prerace and midrace questions, and the end result will take care of itself.

### 3. Do Adjust the Weather Reports

Ten years separated my best and worst marathons. Both came at Boston. If anything, I was better trained for the worst one than the best. The difference was 40 degrees of temperature.

In 1967 we ran through freezing rain. I didn't feel my numbed hands and ears from the start until an hour after I finished. But my legs worked beautifully in this cold.

The day didn't seem hot as we lined up in 1977. It was nothing like the year before, when the mid-90s temperature made us give up on goals and run for fun. The 1977 weather let us keep our racing ambitions, then sneaked up to burn us out later. My last mile took 12 minutes.

The worst heat isn't the 100-degree kind but the kind you don't notice as you stand on the line. The 70- to 80- degree days are the sneakiest, because they feel okay as you stand still. You think you have them beaten. Then the temperature seems to shoot up by 20 degrees as you run.

The thermometer lies to runners, so don't believe what it reads. Use the 20-degree formula: the temperature feels 20 degrees warmer when you run. For example, a 70-degree day is effectively 90, 80 is 100, and so on. The warming factor also works on cold days, making a chilly 30 into a nice 50. Read the long-range weather forecasts, automatically adjust all temperatures upward by 20 degrees, and allow for this as you race. Don't get caught out in the heat.

## 4. Do Plot Your Course

I ran my fastest marathon without seeing any of the course before the race. I raced blind, and about the only thing I liked about the run was the result. I don't recommend racing this way.

It isn't a matter of getting lost. Race courses are well marked and policed, and there are plenty of people to follow. It's *feeling* lost that I don't like. I feel lost when I haven't seen the course in advance.

So I recommend a prerace scouting mission. At least drive the course. Run parts or all of it if you can. Feel the surface; plot the size and location of hills; notice major landmarks; and mark the possible trouble-spots in your mind.

Don't try to memorize exact distances or street names at turns. Officials take care of those checkpoints for you. Just try to make yourself feel at home on the course. This will help you for two reasons. First, distances on familiar routes somehow seem shorter than those in strange places. Second, you avoid nasty surprises like a mile-long hill no one bothered mentioning on the entry blank.

## 5. Don't Leave Logistics to Chance

The best training programs and racing plans don't mean much if you don't get to the starting line on time. The best result loses its glamour if you stand at the finish line with no place to go and no one to help you.

I can't count the times I've looked for a school or park that no gas station attendant knew how to find. I haven't missed many starts, but I've started plenty of races without checking in or warming up. This is a terrible thing to do to an already agitated mind and body.

It is terrible to leave a tired mind and body standing around after a race. This always happened to me at the finish of the Bay-to-Breakers, where the start and finish are 7½ miles apart. The ocean breeze sucked the thrill of the race out of me, replacing it with a chill, as I tried to bum a ride back to my car at the start.

So, my advice is to make travel plans early, including any reservations you need. Check all routes in advance, particularly the exact location of the start. Ask someone who isn't running to drive for you, and have him meet you at the end with clothes, drinks, praise, and a ride home.

### 6. Don't Change Shoes or Clothes

My feet were trying to tell me something, though it was a long time before I listened. I ran my first marathon in the heaviest shoes I've ever worn. Later, I thought I could cut time by reducing shoe weight, so I wore shoes half as bulky as the old ones. I never improved. I gave away too much cushioning for the sake of lightness. Worse, I sacrificed support. Each time I switched to a floppier, lower-heeled "racing flat," my feet hurt for days.

I don't change shoes for races anymore and don't advise you to do it. The risk is too great. The time when you put the most stress on your feet is not the time to make them adapt to a new footfall. Two tips: (1) race in everyday running shoes you know won't hurt you; and (2) never break in new shoes of any kind in a race. The guiding principle here is the same for everything you wear—shoes and clothing: wear nothing in races until it has passed the tests of both your longest and fastest training runs.

### 7. Don't Eat to Run Better

Eating is like training. You aren't going to help yourself much in the last week, but it isn't too late to do some harm.

Before you say, "But what about carbohydrate-loading; isn't that done in the last week, and doesn't it help?" I'll tell you about the diet-juggling technique.

Carbohydrate-loading apparently does no good for races lasting less than an hour, and little good for anything shorter than a marathon. The chances of doing it wrong and wrecking a race are greater than the chances of benefitting from it. (The bad side-effects include psychological upsets and lowered resistance to infection in the depletion phase, as well as weight gain and a bloated feeling during loading.)

Forget the tricks. Forget about eating or drinking anything

you haven't already tested before training and found to be okay. In fact, you might even forget about eating as often or as much as usual this last week. You're training less, so you might gain weight at a time you need to stay slim. You might be the nervous type who reacts against some foods and would be better off not eating anything for 8 to 12 hours before races.

Taper off your eating as you taper your training. Eat lightly and cautiously. Eat without thinking what it might do to improve your running; eat only to avoid slowing it.

### 8. Don't Lose Too Much Sleep

Folk wisdom tells us it's not last night's sleep that gets us through today; it's the sleep we had the *night before last.* We drag through Monday with half-closed eyes as payment for Saturday night's late party.

My experience with sleepless nights before races bears out the wisdom of this. When I took races seriously, I ran them all night. If I slept at all, the dreams were more tiring than lying awake. I never noticed feeling any more tired on race day. But if I lost sleep one night earlier or had to race two days in a row, I was in trouble. The message is clear: sleep normally two nights before the race, then don't worry if you sleep fitfully the last night.

This pattern has significance for training, too. Its effects are delayed, so you often feel more sore and tired two days after a hard run than you feel the next day. As you taper your training, then, make the next-to-last day the easiest one. Give yourself every chance to start fresh.

### Self-Test 7

### What Are You Doing This Week?

1.  Have you cut your training time or mileage in as much as half this last week? Have you taken extra short, easy runs?

2.  Have you thought through your moves, from your arrival at the race site through at least the first pace checkpoint?

3.  Have you checked the weather forecast for race day? Have you added 20 degrees to the predicted temperature?

4.  Have you studied the course you'll run? Have you noted the trouble-spots and how you'll handle them?

5.  Have you made travel plans? Have you checked the maps? Have you estimated time schedules and left enough time to get there comfortably?

6.  Have your shoes and clothes passed all training tests? Have you packed them for the race?

7.  Have you decided not to vary your diet radically this week, and not to overeat?

8.  Have you scheduled a good night's sleep two nights before the race?

Note: The proper answer to each of these is "yes." The corresponding numbered section in this chapter provides the rationale for each.

# 8

## The Last Hours

You wake up, stand on the forward edge of the day, and try to convince yourself it is a day like any other—24 hours long, with the same sunrise and sunset as always. You do this to calm yourself, just as you might say, "Eight hundred million Chinese have no idea what I'm about to do and wouldn't care if they did know."

But it doesn't work. *You* know and care that today is "the day"—race day. It is a day of mystery, of anticipation, of dread. You made yourself a promise about this day months ago. You counted down the days as you trained for it. You'll bore your grandchildren with stories of what you did today. But what will you do today? You can't know until you race, of course, so you wait . . . and wonder . . . and worry. Each minute between you and the race yawns like an hour. This is your longest day.

You're on edge and in doubt. You feel the urge to do something, anything, but you aren't sure what. Uneasiness leads to aimless motion, confusion to mistakes. Since you neither want to waste motion today nor to make mistakes, you need a plan. Design your plan before the day arrives, and make it simple enough so you follow it automatically in the last hours.

I can't promise that any of this will give a second's improvement in your racing result. But I do know it guides you through constructive, necessary actions at a time when you aren't sure you can remember to tie your shoes.

### 1. Get Up Early

Scientists have confirmed what most of us already knew.

50

They tested athletic performances at different times of day. The best results came in late afternoon, and the poorest in early morning. They relate this to *circadian rhythms,* which simply means we feel better after we've been out of bed awhile. We know that from training. Early-morning runners know better than anyone what it is to be sore, stiff, and tired. We hobble from the bed to the bathroom, start our runs on six-inch strides, and need a half-hour to blow the sleep from our heads. Only then does running start to flow as it should. Even then, the overall pace is half a minute per mile slower than it would be in the afternoon with equal effort.

You may have to jump from bed into running shoes to train. But you must not race that way. You risk injury by racing while stiff and sore, and you surely give away too much time. Most distance races are scheduled in the morning, some very early. So get up several hours earlier, even if it means beating dawn. Take a walk in the fresh air to wake and loosen yourself up. (You probably had a restless night, anyway, and welcome the chance to move.) You won't miss the lost hours in bed if it means saving some minutes in the race.

### 2. Stay Close to the Bathroom

The reason should be obvious: your bladder and bowels are twice as busy as usual. This extra activity is part of race day, so don't worry about the amount. Just make sure you have a place to put it.

I've never been to a race yet that had enough toilets for everyone. Don't expect your event to be any different. Go as often as you can before leaving home, and then stop along the way. Don't hold off until you arrive at the check-in area, then wait in line behind a dozen runners with the same needs. If the waiting doesn't bother you, the messy toilets will. (It seems to be a rule that they must clog and overflow before you get there.) I rarely use the official facilities. I go back to nature when nature calls. Nearby woods, like those surrounding the high school near the start of the Boston Marathon, have no waiting lines. Don't be modest. You don't want to carry anything to the starting line that might want out as you run.

### 3. Eating is Optional

I never eat the morning of a race. This isn't a fast before battle, or an attempt to make myself feel lean and mean. I'm just not hungry, and I know I don't need anything. I know I run on what went through my digestive system and was stored in my muscles yesterday, not what I put into my stomach on race day. New food might cause trouble now; no food causes no problems.

Do whatever you normally do. If you typically run in the morning, as I do, eight to twelve hours or more after last eating, race that way. Don't eat. You know you won't collapse from malnutrition at the halfway point. If you're used to eating before running, consume an amount you know you can tolerate. Realize, though, that all you're doing is filling a hole; you aren't getting much new energy this late. Barely satisfy the hunger with light carbohydrates that won't lie there to haunt you later.

### 4. Drinking Is Essential

Even on cool days, runners throw off liquids at an alarming rate. This starts before the race, for reasons I gave in point two. So you might already be down a quart or so as you start.

The race itself costs as much as a gallon of sweat. You may take drinks en route, but you gain back only a fraction of the five to ten pounds of lost liquid. This drain affects performance in cool weather, and health in hot weather.

Fluid loss while running is inevitable. But you don't have to give it a headstart. Drink your way to the starting line, making sure you replace much of what your nerves have flushed out.

What to drink? Some runners recommend tea, coffee, and even beer, but these may speed up the flushing action. Fruit juices may react badly in a nervous stomach. Heavily sugared drinks tend to keep water in the stomach, away from where it is needed. Body Punch and Gookinaid, drinks designed for runners, are effective. Plain water is safest. Whatever you drink, take small amounts, often.

### 5. Remember Shoes and Shorts

The simplest things are the ones most easily forgotten. Many's the time I have heard a runner wail, "My God, I brought two left shoes! Please, does anyone have an extra pair of size 9½ New Balance 320s?" I've seen runners walk to the line, pull down their warmup bottoms, and find they wore only a jock-strap underneath.

Put on your shorts and shoes at home, and wear them to the race. That way, you know you have your two key items. You can borrow any old shirt if you forget that, and you don't need anything else. Don't take any other clothes or equipment that you can't afford to lose. You'll have to leave this at the start, and it may not be there when you return. I now wear old Levis and a $5 Windbreaker from K-Mart. One lost or stolen set of fancy sweats taught me the wisdom of traveling cheaply and lightly.

### 6. Arrive Early if You Drive

Know your route, find someone to take you, and allow plenty of time. I've given this travel advice already (see chapter 7).

Travel is so draining that I never again want to spend more than an hour at it on race day. (I have driven six times that far on occasion.) If the trip is longer, and particularly if the race starts early in the morning, I'd rather go the day before and stay overnight. Racing is hard enough without adding the burden of highway fatigue.

If you must travel the same day you race, allow time after arrival to shake out the kinks from the trip. Give yourself an extra hour beyond the time you need for warming up.

### 7. Sign Up First

One of the happier trends in distance racing is early check-in. You register before a deadline, then pick up your number or get it in the mail days before the event. So there is no waiting in line on race day. However, don't count on this happening all the time. Part of being a racer is enduring frustrating waits as officials take care of paperwork.

Do your waiting in line as soon as you can and as little as you must. Line up at the check-in tables before you start to warm up. Don't interrupt your prerace concentration for this. Pick a time when the crowds are small, get in the shortest line, do your business, then hurry away to a calmer place.

### 8. Sample the Course

I told you in the last chapter to check it all, carefully, running it if possible. Now, I suggest walking or just standing and looking at the small parts of it; don't run. The varying advice is for different days. Race day is too late for a complete tour. Take that in the days before, or else not at all. This also relates to nerves. Your confidence is shaky enough without exposing it to every mile and hill. Distances seem twice as long and climbs twice as high now as they will when you race them, so save them for later.

Just know where the starting line is (and the finish if it is different). Check how you come in at the end, when you may be alone and confused. Ask the locations of the major hills, time checkpoints, and aid stations, without actually going to see them. If you have a choice, warm up away from the course and all of its people.

### 9. Avoid the Crowds

I'm a talker. I go to races as much for social reasons as athletic ones. But the time to be sociable is *after* I race. Before, I don't feel like talking. I brush off old friends as quickly as courtesy will allow, and I detour around people I know only slightly. This is a time for concentrating, not conversing.

Part of warming up for a race is simply thinking about it. You think best alone. If you have time after arriving and checking in, go away alone and rest. When the active part of warming up begins, do it by yourself, too.

Even if you don't want to be a loner, others may. Respect their privacy. You'll have plenty to talk about later.

### 10.  Start Hot or Stay Cool?

The amount of warmup you need depends on the distance you race. The shorter and faster the event, the more you must run before it starts; the longer it is, the less preliminary running you need.

Think what goes on in training. You're awkward at first. Your stiff legs resist motion. Your breathing is ragged. Then, at 5 to 10 minutes, sweating starts. Another 5 to 10 minutes later, your muscles loosen and breathing smooths. A little more time, and running finally feels the way it should. You go faster without trying harder. It has taken nearly a half-hour to get there.

Now, think how you would have felt if the race hadn't lasted that long. It would have been awful! You never would have warmed up. The lesson is to start hot if the race is short. Before a mile race, for instance, run what amounts to a full workout. Run for a half-hour, stop for a few minutes to walk and do stretching exercises, and then take two or three 30-second accelerations to top racing speed.

However, if the race is a marathon, stay cool. Take no running warmup; only walk and stretch. Start running slowly when the gun sounds, using the first few miles to warm up. This is a small part of the race distance, and you will lose little time here. Running this part cold helps you resist the urge of most marathoners to start too fast and lose lots more time at the other end.

Adjust the amount of warmup to the racing distance and speed. Use the "full workout" plan before any race lasting less than 30 minutes, about half that amount to prepare for races of 30-60 minutes, and little or nothing for races longer than an hour.

### Self-Test 8
### What Are You Doing Today?

1. Do you know why you should get out of bed at dawn, even though your race doesn't start until mid-morning?

2. Do you understand why you may be going to the bathroom once each hour?

3. Do you accept the fact that you need to eat little or nothing today, and can run well without it?

4. Do you know why you should drink more today than you usually do?

5. Do you have on, or at least have packed, your shorts and (a matched pair of) shoes?

6. Do you plan to travel less than two hours on race day and arrive in time to rest from the trip?

7. Have you picked a time to wait in line to check in that will upset you least?

8. Do you know the main features of the course—start, finish, checkpoints, hills, etc.?

9. Do you feel the need to get away from friends and be alone, or see the need to leave them alone?

10. Do you appreciate the need to warm up a long time for short races and very little for long races?

Note: "Yes" is the correct answer to these questions. Check the corresponding numbers in the text for the reasons.

# 9

# You Should Be Scared

There, I've started and I feel better already. I was scared. I had prepared well for this. I'd done this hundreds of times before. It should get easier to face with experience, but it has never grown easier. Each time I start, it's as if I'm a rookie.

All the familiar signs were there again today: the gnawing in my guts, the urge to visit the john once more, the pounding in my head, the weakness, the confusion, and the wish to be anywhere but here doing anything but this. I felt too puny to ascend this mountain I had to climb.

But I started. I squeezed my eyes shut at the last second, gulped my heart from my throat back down into my chest, and took the first step. I'm better now.

I'm writing about writing. These paragraphs tell how I felt as I faced this chapter this morning. I balked at putting down the first words on clean paper, as I always balk. Yet I know this fear is important—not pleasant, but normal and necessary to get me ready to do anything beyond ordinary scribbles. Fear makes me work better.

This is the mind's way of readying the body (and vice versa) for any kind of emergency: picking a fight, facing a boss, delivering a speech, or running a race. Fear gets the juices flowing. These juices, in turn, fuel harder, sharper, more concentrated efforts than we otherwise could make.

Athletes call it "psyching up." It works like magic. There's no other word I can use to explain why I rarely run even half a marathon at eight minutes per mile in practice, but race the full distance at a sub-seven-minute pace. Magic.

On a much higher plane, Frank Shorter has said he couldn't possibly force himself to go even 10-15 miles at less than five minutes each in training. It would exhaust him. But he races this way for 26-plus miles. He credited "the excitement of the race" for the difference.

We think of the excitement only in its thrilling sense. We don't consider another side of it—fear. Anticipation and dread work together to put us on alert. Anticipation is pleasant, so I need to say no more about it, except enjoy it. Dread is the worrisome part. I can't make it go away and wouldn't if I could. I can't make you like it. All I can do is help you understand how it feels and why, and help you see it as a friend in disguise.

Ron Hill, one of the all-time great long-distance runners, called it "a useful kind of fear. This is a good thing to develop, you know. It keeps you moving."

Know the normal patterns and how to react to them. First, anticipation gives way to dread in the last 24 hours or so, when you have time to sit, wait, and think about what you're going to do to yourself.

The waiting is the worst part. You can't wait to get started, yet you don't know if you want to start—or will be able. The last hours drag along, and a troubled mind fills them with a month's worth of worrying. You seem to examine every thought and movement with a microscope.

"Should I eat this? It might upset my stomach."

"Oh, no. My shorts are rubbing. What will this do to my crotch after a couple of miles?"

"God, I've got to get some rest. How can I run if I can't keep my eyes open?"

"My left shoe has a flaw. Will my skin survive the race?"

"Nausea! Could it be the start of the flu?"

"Uh-oh, a twinge in my calf!"

"Diarrhea. What if I don't get it all out and have to stop in mid-race—or can't stop in time?"

"Is that the wind I hear?"

"Look how fit and relaxed all the other runners are. I'm so wasted I can't go 100 yards with them."

Don't trust any judgments, and try not to make any big

decisions. You aren't in enough control of your rational mind. Make all your plans ahead of time, and then go mechanically through the motions of carrying them out. (See chapter 8 for specifics.) Make a ritual of this.

Robert F. Jones of *Sports Illustrated* once wrote of prerace reactions, and the rituals he used to deal with them. He went back to relive his glory as a swimmer after fifteen years away from the sport. Instead of the glory, he rediscovered long-suppressed feelings of fear and dread. Jones recalled:

> At first, it was only a flicker, a brief preoccupation, a butterfly emerging from its cocoon. I helped it along with some of the old rituals: a few curses, as obscene as I could make them, directed not only against my opponents and my coach, but against myself for letting me get into so grave a confrontation.
>
> The butterfly grew stronger with every obscenity. I fed it further with a mug of hot, strong tea, so thickly laced with honey you could feel it in your wrist when you stirred. I hadn't shaved or brushed my teeth that day, another of the old rituals. Makes you meaner and stronger, we used to believe.

Jones used the right word: *ritual.* Habitual ways of eating, dressing, thinking, and acting on race day may be laughed off as superstitions by anyone but a befuddled runner who needs familiar things to hold onto before plunging into the unknown. The race scares you with both its knowns and unknowns. You know it will hurt, no matter how you run it. You know it holds surprises, but you are left to guess what types of surprises and where they will appear. It's like knowing you are about to be mugged, without knowing exactly when or how badly. You cling to friends as you wait.

Most of the time, waiting for the first blow to land feels far worse than any blows in the race—probably because prerace fear acts later as an anaesthetic. The body and mind get ready for racing with reactions the scientists call "fight-or-flight responses." These are biological-psychological warmup exercises for stressful encounters. You know the stress mechanism is working when you feel any of the 13 symptoms offered by Scottish sports doctor A. M. D. MacIntyre:

1. dryness of mouth, often called "cotton-mouth"
2. stomach distress—an unsettled feeling, often accompanied by decreased appetite and in some cases vomiting

3. heavy perspiration

4. frequent urination and mild diarrhea

5. deeper, more rapid breathing

6. faster, stronger heartbeat

7. tense, tight muscles—particularly in the neck and shoulder area

8. overall feeling of weakness and lethargy

9. pale complexion

10. fingernail biting and other unconscious hand-occupying actions

11. irritability and restlessness, along with difficulty getting to sleep and staying asleep

12. withdrawal from social contacts

13. desire to escape the event at hand, and to establish excuses in advance for failing to perform up to expectations

Expect these signs and accept them. A little fear is nothing to be afraid of.

### Self-Test 9
### How Do You Feel?

1.    Are you eager to get started rather than having mixed feelings about what you must do?

2.    Are you confident that things will go right, instead of worrying about little things that might go wrong?

3.    Did you sleep as soundly as normal last night?

4.    Do you feel wide awake, alert, strong, and energetic enough for the work ahead?

5.    Are you free of aches and pains, and of worries that these will affect your running?

6.    Have you made your usual number of visits to the rest room today?

7. Are you able to sit for an hour without fidgeting or finding excuses to get up and move?

8. As you sit there, check the muscles of your shoulders and gut. Are they loose and relaxed?

9. Are you able to carry on an intelligent conversation in which the subject of the race doesn't come up?

10. Can you concentrate for more than a few minutes on any thought that doesn't concern your race?


Note: Ask yourself these questions in the final hours before the race. If your nervousness is building normally, I'd expect you to answer "no" to most of them.

# 10

## Running with People

George Sheehan tells better than I can about competition at its best. The sport's philosopher-in-residence writes: "I was in the final mile of a cross-country race when I heard him coming up on my shoulder. We were part of a rather small field, perhaps 80 in all. Only a few were accomplished runners. Most had come to see the benefits of running lately. For them—and I'm sure for him—a five-mile race was a new experience."

As the younger, stronger man pulled alongside and then ahead, Sheehan called, "Way to go! You're looking great!"

George says, "Until he challenged me, I had been running to survive, thinking I was doing the best I could do. Now, I discovered reserves I had not suspected were there. When I finished, I was clocked in my best time of the year."

He says such encounters are "the rule rather than a rarity in running. They embody the essence of the running experience. The young man, nevertheless, found my encouragement almost incomprehensible. The idea than an opponent would urge you to beat him seemed an impossibility. He became so psyched up, he said, he ran better than he had thought possible."

This is the best kind of competition, because you don't have to push anyone down to stand taller. You draw strength from others without draining any of theirs. Sheehan outlines the "racer's creed":

> I am in control of what I do. What I do is me, no one else. In a race, my performance is my concern, not yours. I wish you well. In fact, the better you do, the better I will do as well.
> That is the true nature of competition. The Latin root of the word is *petere*—to go out, to head for, to seek. The *com* is doing it

together, in common, in unity, in harmony. Competition is simply each of us seeking our absolute best with the help of each other. What we do magnifies each other, inspires each of us.

In this setting, Sheehan finds it "unintelligible to cheat anyone else or to be diminished by the performance of another."

If I can draw a Golden Rule of Racing from this, it is: *No one can beat you but you.* That means you don't have to look at other racers as "the enemy." They are there to make you run harder, longer, faster than any of you could go alone. You try your damnedest to beat them to the finish, of course, but you know you're only using them to help you beat the only competitor who counts—yourself.

You feel none of the hatred some athletes must conjure up against their opponents. You feel no need to use physical and psychological tricks on them. You want to get from the start to the end as fast as possible, and interfering with anyone else's race would only slow your own. Your sole "tactic" is to find the fastest path. This is the ideal way of looking at racing. We're all in it together, helping each other. I'm ashamed to say my reality hasn't always lived up to that ideal.

I was taking the last part of my weekly long run with racers in a four-mile. While they pushed, I just loafed along. That was my first mistake. I wasn't in the race on everyone else's terms, so I shouldn't have been there at all. I acted superior to the people around me who worked while I coasted. Occasionally, I threw in a burst of speed. As I spurted away from some runners and rushed past others, I could almost hear them thinking, "What a hot dog!"

With the end of the run closing in, I heard footsteps behind me. I looked back to see a boy in glasses. I judged him to be about sixteen and not too fit. His head was down, and his arms flailed as he sprinted hard to catch me. He hadn't run a very good race, but here was his chance to finish it well as his faster teammates watched. They cheered for him to pass me.

I kicked, too, but the boy kept coming. His buddies yelled louder. As I felt him coming on my right, I veered to that side of the road—all the way to the outside—to keep him behind me. He cut his stride and tried to go to my left. I veered in that direction. I still led as it ended.

After we finished, I looked back. The boy was hanging over

a fence, glaring at me. He gasped, "That . . . was . . . dirty-pool . . . running me . . . off the road . . . like that."

And it was. I'd deliberately done what I've spent much of my writing career telling others to avoid. For all my talk about helping runners, I'd stood in one runner's way.

The truth about racing falls between George Sheehan's example and mine. We don't always love our fellow racers as brothers, but we rarely stand in their way. Most of the time, we just mind our manners. That's all sportsmanship is: good manners. Without these courtesies, races would dissolve into street fights.

Running is a sport of few rules and many customs. This is a nice arrangement for the sport, because it needs few officials to enforce its minimal written rules. The runners themselves do most of their own policing with their customs.

These are the rights and wrongs of racing. They are the glue that holds together the fragile alliance among the three groups who make organized racing possible: the participants, the promoters, and the people who control the facilities we use. Our dealings with each other are no more or less than the good manners that are part of the sport's tradition.

A Chicago police office once said after watching a road race with 5,000 entrants, "This is the largest crowd in the city's history without a harsh word being said. Nobody is accusing anybody. Nobody is denouncing someone else. Nobody is mad. It's just a quiet, pleasant event."

Running couldn't operate on its present large scale if we weren't this orderly. As long as we all follow a simple code of behavior toward each other and the race promoters, the sport runs smoothly.

## Fellow Racers

The basic advice is: don't interfere or intentionally disturb another runner's pace and concentration.

**Start where you expect to finish.** At a crowded starting line, choose a spot that matches where you'll be at the end. If you're average, start in the middle of the pack; if fast, the front; if slow, the back. Don't force faster runners to climb over you to find running room. Don't handicap yourself by waiting for slower runners to clear the line ahead of you.

**Pass cleanly.** Be sure you have room to go around. Make no contact as you pass. Don't cross in front of the runner you pass until you are two or more strides ahead of him. If someone blocks your way and has room to move over, shout for the right of way. Most runners are glad to yield.

**Yield to the faster runner.** When someone tries to pass, by all means give him a fair fight. (The definition of *fair* doesn't include throwing elbows or veering across his path to hold him back.) If you're being lapped on a track or on a repeating course, move out to let the lapper through on the inside.

**Finish what you start.** Never begin a race planning to drop out along the way, or planning to jump into one in the middle "for a workout." This isn't fair to runners who pace along with you, assuming you're going all the way as they are.

**Speak only if spoken to.** You can, of course, give other runners grunts of recognition or encouragement. But don't force people into conversation en route, and never practice cheap psych-out tricks like telling someone how bad he looks. Concentration and confidence are fragile during a race.

## Officials and Others

The key words here are: be tolerant and patient with officials. Handling races is a big, thankless job, usually performed by volunteers or half-hearted recruits. Don't make their job harder than it already is, or they won't show up next time.

Remember, too, that we share the places where we run. Other people use them. Others often control them and can take them away from us if we abuse our privileges.

**Pay or stay out of the way.** You should go through the approved entry process, but many runners don't. If you run unofficially, don't spoil things for the promoters and the runners who paid to be there. Don't get in their way at the start, take their drinks, or—most importantly—cross the finish line and mess up everyone's results.

**Cooperate with the officials.** Arrive and check in early. Get to the starting line on time. Follow directions en route. Get away from the chaotic finish area as soon as you've finished running. Wait until everyone is finished before asking for your time and place. Thank the officials if their work deserves it.

**Follow the rules of the road.** If the road is open to auto traffic, don't interfere with it (or risk your own life) by running in mid-road, on the right side (the *wrong* side for a pedestrian), or zig-zagging across the road. Stay on the left unless directed otherwise.

**Be friendly to the natives.** Don't run them down, as they use the same paths. Respect their property; don't use their yards as a dressing room or toilet. Smile and wave if they say something nice to you.

**Clean up after yourself.** Several hundred runners, each dropping a postrace drink, can leave behind a lot of garbage.

### Self-Test 10
### How Are Your Manners?

1. Do you think of competition essentially as a racer of "me against him," which only one of you can win?

2. Do you find it necessary to view other racers as "the enemy"?

3. Do you feel intimidated by running against stronger, faster people? Does running with such people seem to diminish your performance?

4. Do you have to knock someone else down, literally or figuratively, to make yourself feel taller?

5. Do you consider it a surrender to say, "Looking good! Way to go!" when a runner passes you?

6. Do you think anyone ever really beats you except yourself?

7. Do you think anyone in the race really cares how you do except yourself?

8. Do you always see it as your right to be on the front row at the start, then to hold the inside lane at all costs?

9. Do you think it's an accepted part of the game to block the path of runners who try to pass?

10. Do you assume the streets belong only to runners on race day, and that walkers and drivers must yield to you?

Note: These should be "no" answers.

# 11

# Running with Time

Erratic pacing breaks hearts. Even pacing breaks records. Runners who want to win races from other people may need to use the first tactic. But since you aren't trying to break anyone else's heart with fancy pacing tricks—and since the heart you break will more likely be your own—I promote only the second tactic. Steady pacing, the kind that breaks your records, has the most dramatic effect on race results of anything you do, other than training. Yet it is a skill rarely perfected, even by runners who know its value. The classic style of racing works against good pacing.

"Survival of the fittest" is the way most distance races are run—indeed, the way racing is taught in the schools. Coaches tell young runners to stay with the leaders; "maintain contact." Once you lose contact, they say, you're dead—not bothering to mention that you probably will drop if you try to keep it up, too. This gives track and cross-country racing a pattern that carries over to some extent to the roads.

It's a mile. At the end of the first quarter, all 15 runners are bunched within a few yards. At the half, five have dropped off and are slipping back. At three-quarters, five more have fallen away from the front-runners. Three more slip away on the backstretch. Now, coming off the final turn, two milers are left. The strongest and fastest of the two wins the race for the tape.

A good race, you might say. Sure it was—for the leaders who could handle the pace. But what about the other 10 who tried to keep up, but couldn't? They started too fast for their abilities. They lost contact—and probably fighting spirit with it—and ended up shuffling home slower than if they'd let the leaders get away at the start.

Dreams of glory are fine, front-running is fine—if you are good enough to carry it through. In any race, however, only a few runners can maintain a front-running pace. Most are hurt by it.

Arthur Lydiard, coach of several world record-holders in New Zealand, wrote more than fifteen years ago, "The ideal starting pace is the pace one knows he can maintain all the way. Only among top athletes who are fighting for championship honors should it be necessary for tactics to enter into it. Between them, fast takeoffs in an attempt to break up the field are expected and warranted. But we take good care to warn a less ambitious runner not to get tangled up in this sort of cut-throat running. He is the one whose throat will be cut first."

Even if you don't let delusions of grandeur run away with you, even if you ignore the leaders, you'll probably still start too fast if you follow your legs. They are fresh and eager. They want to go and go hard, now! But don't let them—not yet, anyway. You have to conserve during times of plenty for the energy famine that is sure to come later. Good racing goes against your nature. You must hold back when you feel like breaking loose, and then push when you want to ease off.

This is the basic law of pacing. Arthur Lydiard quoted it when he told milers, "The best way to get the full benefit of ability in the mile is to go out with the attitude that it is a half-mile race and, as far as you're concerned, the time to start putting on the pressure is when the first half-mile is behind you."

This pattern applies to all races: start *cautiously*—not slowly, but keep speed in careful check. Then open up the reserve power systems after the halfway point. Make every race two races, each the same in size, but very different in style.

Run the first half as a "pacer." Ignore the people around you who dash away from the starting line; keep your head as they lose theirs. Run like a scientist, with coolness, wisdom, and restraint, following a safe pacing plan you set up in advance, making small corrections as needed. You quietly do a job. You set a stage for the time when real racing begins.

That begins at about halfway. Here, you change your style completely. Run the second half as a "racer." Use the runners around you to pull you along. Run like an artist, an actor who bares his guts and emotions. Throw away inhibitions, forget time schedules, and race spontaneously with all you have left. If the pacer/scientist does his job, the racer/artist can run an inspired race. If not, the mistakes of the first half spoil the performance in the second.

Several years ago, while editing the booklet *Racing Techniques,* I checked the world records. I compared the halves of those races and figured how far the paces varied from even. The results:

- One man—Kerry O'Brien in the steeplechase—ran exactly even times.

- The majority of records—18 of 25—were run with the second half slower than the first, but the time difference in almost every case was only a few seconds per mile.

- The other six record-setters finished faster than they started. They had what swimmers call *negative splits.* But again, the differences were small.

The "safety factor" in record races seemed to be five seconds per mile. The pace of the halves varied by more than that amount in only a couple of instances. Most of the records have been improved since 1972, but the record-setting pattern hasn't changed.

The fastest racers still run the steadiest paces. If they started a lot faster than they finished, they would lose more speed in the last half than they had put in the bank in the first. However, if they had dropped too far behind even pace early, they couldn't regain all that time later.

The half-times don't need to be dead even. But the evidence is pretty good that they must stay within the safety range of five seconds per mile of each other for best results. That gives a maximum difference of five seconds between the two 880s of a mile, no more than 30 seconds between the 3-mile halves of a 6-miler or 2.2 minutes between the 13.1-mile halves of a marathon.

## Table 2
## Safety Factors

| Mile Distance | Time Difference | Metric Distance | Time Difference |
|---|---|---|---|
| Mile | 5 sec. | 1,500 m. | 5 sec. |
| 2 miles | 10 sec. | 2,000 m. | 6 sec. |
| 3 miles | 15 sec. | 3,000 m. | 9 sec. |
| 4 miles | 20 sec. | 5,000 m. | 15 sec. |
| 5 miles | 25 sec. | 10,000 m. | 31 sec. |
| 6 miles | 30 sec. | 15,000 m. | 48 sec. |
| 10 miles | 50 sec. | 20,000 m. | 1:02 |
| 15 miles | 1:15 | 25,000 m. | 1:17 |
| 20 miles | 1:40 | 30,000 m. | 1:33 |
| Marathon | 2:10 | 50,000 m. | 2:35 |

Note: The difference in time between the first half of the race and the second shouldn't exceed these amounts (based on five seconds per mile). When projecting race paces, divide your time goal in half, then split the "safety margin" equally on either side of the halfway time to show the fastest and slowest you can start.

The safety range isn't only for world record-setters. It's even more important to those of us trying for personal marks, because we have less basic speed, less training background, and less to gain from heart-breaking changes of pace.

I didn't learn this formula until 500 races were behind me—including all of my personal records. Since I didn't know any better, my paces were all over the clock. However, I now look at my best races and see a remarkably consistent pattern to them.

I have 10 records for standard racing distances between 880 yards and 50 kilometers. The average difference in the half-times was just four-tenths of a second per mile. In one, my 6-mile record, the first- and last-half times were identical. Four ended faster than they began, and two slowed in the second half while staying within the five-seconds-per-mile safety range. The three outside of that range were extreme distances—880, marathon, and 50 kilometers—for which I hadn't done enough speed or endurance training.

My training suited me for events of 1 to 20 miles. In my twenty-five best races at these distances, twenty-three of the splits fell within the safety range and the others were less than a second outside. They all averaged two-tenths of a second faster for the last half than the first.

So I suggest you pace yourself in the following way: Plan the first half, and then let the second half just happen. Base the plan on what you have run before. Adjust it to your present condition and the racing conditions (weather, terrain, etc.). Analyze your times after the race to see if you paced the planned half too fast or too slowly. (The time for the unplanned half will show the result quite clearly.) Then, correct the starting pace the next time you race this distance.

If the distance is new to you and you can't estimate its pace from other races, just start comfortably. Choose what feels like too slow a pace instead of too fast. You'll make up much of the lost time later and feel better about the first experience. This gives you a pacing standard, and you'll be eager to correct it when you race again.

Make the halves very close to the same in time. This doesn't mean, however, that they take the same effort or feel the same speed. You get the sensation of going harder and faster all the way, even as the pace stays constant.

You still are out of step with most other runners, only now the steps favor you. Those runners who let their instincts loose and spurted away from you at the start now wind down. You gather momentum when it counts, because you first held back when that counted.

### Self-Test 11
### What Is Your Best Pace?

**Before the Race**

1.  What is your race distance? (In miles; convert from meters if necessary.)

2.  What time do you expect to run? (Based on past performances at this or other distances; take into account changes in your condition, the weather, terrain, etc.)

3.  What would be even pace for each half? (Divide the expected time by two.)

4. What is the safety factor for this distance? (See the chart or multiply the distance in miles by five seconds per mile.)

5. What is the fastest you should start? (Subtract half of the safety factor from the even-pace figure.)

6. What is the slowest you can start? (Add half of the safety factor to the even-pace figure.)

Note: Use answers 5 and 6 as your guide to pacing.

**After the Race**

1. What time did you run in this race?

2. What was the first-half time? (Estimate by using other known splits if necessary.)

3. What was your second-half time? (Estimate if necessary.)

4. What was the total difference in first-half and second-half times? (Subtract the smaller number from the bigger one.)

5. What was the speedup or slowdown factor per mile? (Divide the number above by the distance of the race in miles.)

6. What would you do differently if you could run the race again? (Start slower, start faster or pace it the same way?)

Note: Use the number in 5 as a guide to answering 6.

# 12

## The Prizes that Count

Two high school teammates walked away from a regional cross-country championship they'd just run. One looked at a mass-produced certificate with a blank space for his name and snarled, "We get all the way here, then they don't give us shit."

The incident reminded me of something similar that happened several months before, when I was working as a scorekeeper at a race. It involved a boy about the same age who thought about the same way. The next day's paper reported, "At 1 a.m., with most of the crowd gone, hurried officials were still trying to sort out the results so they could distribute the awards."

In fact, only one hurried official was figuring. I was the one—I who didn't give a diddlydamn about awards; I who think races should have neither entry fees nor prizes.

I finally sorted out the places and times of the leading runners, the ten who were to get silver bowls. But most of them had gone home without bothering to collect their prizes.

A scarecrow of a boy stuck a popsicle stick in my face. "Here," he said. "I was ninety-seventh. Now, what do I get?"

I was exhausted, and when I'm tired, I'm blunt. I said, "You've already gotten it. A race is its own reward."

He stared blankly, shook his head and walked away. Maybe someday he'll understand what I was trying to say. I was older than he before I understood this.

When I was about this boy's age, I read of Gar Williams. He lived in Chicago then, ran in a lot of long-distance races, and won a good share of them. And he always refused to accept prizes, giving them instead to the next runner in line.

I'd just started to win medals, trophies, and plaques, and each took a place of high honor in the living room shrine. I thought when I read of Williams, "What a noble thing to do!"

I still think the result of Gar's act was noble (that is, giving a prize to someone who wanted and needed it more than he did). But I see now that his motive probably wasn't so much generosity as disinterest in awards. He was sure enough of himself that he didn't need them as a tangible reminder that "I'm special!" The things he earned from racing were less visible and more real.

I lost interest in awards for similar reasons:

- They go to the wrong people. The same 1 percent gets awards week after week, while the runners who need these trinkets to shore up their shaky motivation never take home more than "finisher" certificates and "survivor" ribbons.

- More to the point, the race is as temporary as a spring flower. It blooms for a brief moment, we admire it, and then it withers and dies. We can't make it last. Likewise, race results quickly come and go. Awards try to make permanent a thrill that can only be short-lived.

- Most important, the reward is the race itself. Awards are only cheap symbols of what happened there. No one needs idols of wood, metal, and plastic to tell him he ran well, and no prize makes up for a race run poorly.

Many runners share these sentiments with me. But this doesn't change the fact that far more runners want and need awards. I'm not referring here to mass awards—the kind everyone gets at road races. Such awards simply show you were part of the crowd; they make no comment on your ability to do anything more than finish the prescribed number of miles. Something-for-everyone awards cause a few problems—like greedy stampedes on the distributors of "free" T-shirts or inflated entry fees to pay for all the goodies. But the simplicity and honesty of the sport take much more of a beating from overemphasis on the rewards that only a few runners can earn.

Ambitious runners who want solid evidence that "I'm special!" have always been with us. As running grows, there are more of them. Their number seems to grow faster than the number of worthwhile victories available. But don't underestimate the imagination of anyone with ambition. If he can't win on the old terms, he'll make up new ones to suit himself. New divisions within races, new record categories, even new events are all ways of substituting with imagination for what one lacks in talent. This is also true of artificial equalizers, such as handicapping and out and out cheating.

Subdividing races and records is part of the time-honored practice of reducing the size of the pond until you're a large fish swimming in it. Some races list so many divisions, I'm expecting soon to find one for left-handed thirty-five-year-old writers from Iowa with two children.

Bob Anderson, publisher of *Runner's World,* put the brakes on the proliferation of 24-hour relay records by saying, "It was getting so ridiculous, we had everything but a record for a team with a man, a woman, and a dog."

Bob and I exaggerate to make the point that winning races and breaking records should remain special. When too many people claim to be best, they cheapen the results of those who truly are.

Runners who can't get what they want from the normal events may step beyond the norm. (A former co-worker of mine called these "flagpole-sitting records.") They say, if I can't win at your game, I'll start my own. If you run across the United States, I'll run across and back. If you run around the country's borders, I'll run around the world. The feats may be incredible, but they aren't really records until a large number of people standardize them and prove their worth. Few ever do.

Make the usual leaders run backward or hop on one leg. The effect wouldn't be much more dramatic than it is in "handicap" races, which give slower runners a head start. Handicapping is intended to give every runner an equal chance of winning by wiping out the inequalities of age, sex, genes, and training. But its real effect is to penalize people for racing well and to make the others imagine they are something they aren't. Competition is meant to help people see their true abilities, not to mask their differences.

The most seriously troubled competitors are those who need

to win so desperately that they cheat. A national Masters (ages forty and up) champion and record-holder was exposed as a fraud one summer. He'd added five years to his age to qualify for the Masters meets. Through the years, *Runner's World* has detected several runners who report false race results that show themselves winning in spectacular times. I could name names, but won't. They have enough problems already.

All of this has something to do with the "Guinness Syndrome," named after the world-record book. This syndrome is a drive for success and recognition so powerful that one will go to ludicrous extremes to find ways of "achieving" them. This is a fantasy land where every word ends in "-est": biggest, fastest, longest, highest, best. Everything is compared and ranked—and prizes are a way of keeping score.

We'll all do ourselves and the sport a favor if we wipe out of our thinking the idea that running is only worth doing if we're best at it and have something tangible to show for the effort afterward. Dr. Thomas Tutko, a noted sports psychologist, explains limits of this: "The emphasis is on the product and not the process. The product is temporary. The trouble with the product is that it always has to be replaced by another one. That's a hell of a way to live."

Runners who struggle to win so they can earn a piece of paper, cloth, metal, wood, or plastic that says "I'm special!" are forgetting that they already are special for having raced at all. Those who play with statistics and rules to make themselves appear unique are only trying to find what others already have: a personal definition of victory that has little to do with finishing position or rewards they can hold.

## Self-Test 12
### What Did You Expect?

1. Did you expect to have your name announced as you finished?

2. Did you expect a standing ovation from the crowd?

3.  Did you expect to be honored for your limitations (of age, sex, etc.)?

4.  Did you expect to be interviewed for television or radio?

5.  Did you expect to see your name (or picture) in the paper the next day?

6.  Did you expect to win a medal (trophy, plaque, merchandise prize)?

7.  Did you expect to capture forever the thrill of the race in a prize you could see and touch?

8.  Did you expect the real prize-winners to be more excited about their awards?

9.  Did you expect more than a piece of paper (or a ribbon) stating you were there and survived?

10. Did you expect more than an accurate time and place?


Note: If you answered "yes" to any of these, you missed the point of this chapter: your race is its own reward; anything you get beyond time and place is a by-product.

# 13

# The Numbers Game

You cross the finish line. One official shouts a time as another records it on a clipboard. You have shut off your digital wrist-stopwatch at the same moment. Now, you check it as you walk away to see if your time matches the one you heard. You accept the faster of the two times. The first thing you must know when you finish the race is, "What is my time?" The second is, "What does it mean?"

Distance, and then time, are the standards that can make winners of us all. The first victory is finishing. The second is running the distance faster than you have before. No one else can do more than finish; no one can beat your personal record.

Time for a distance shows more, however, than what happens here and now. Unlike sports with arbitrary point systems—football, baseball, tennis, golf, and most others—running results cross lines of time and space. Nebraska's football score against Alabama on Saturday tells only how the two teams did against each other that day. It says little about how each might have done against UCLA—or how well they met their own standards of perfection.

Running times don't have these limits. A miler from Nebraska can race against one from Alabama today and know how he might have done against one from Florida racing someplace else. Not only that, but those racing in 1979 can race against marks left behind in 1959. This year's runners can leave records for people to break in the 1980s. Best of all, runners can compete against their own histories and be winners without being first.

Time is your most important result. It not only lets you race this distance with these people now; it allows you to compare your races with all other races at all distances that you and everyone else have ever run. This is why you want to know your time first thing after finishing. This is why you work out its meanings. This is to be a page in your history.

You have your time. Now, start processing it. Get it ready to go into your history book in a form you understand and can compare with earlier and later times.

**First, compare the time with another known standard.** The race may have been at an odd distance like 7.6 miles. Your time of 52:36 doesn't tell you much. So you reduce it to a minutes-per-mile pace if you're American. Almost everyone else in the world uses minutes-per-kilometer, but the math is the same.

You divide 52.6 by 7.6. (The figuring is easier if you convert seconds into tenths of a minute. Six seconds equals one-tenth.) Your pace was 6.92 minutes per mile or 6 minutes, 55 seconds.

Pace means more than overall time, since you judge every training run and race by this standard. You know immediately how much faster you raced per mile than you normally go for a similar distance in training. Or you know how much farther you were able to hold a pace than you do in everyday runs.

If you're like me, when you race you can count on improving your training pace by at least a minute a mile at a short distance, or else holding a training pace for twice the normal distance. Pace-per-mile figures tell you exactly how much better you are in racing than in training.

They also tell you how well you measure up against all runners. Anyone who averages five-minute miles or better for distances longer than a mile or two doesn't need this book; he's a national- or world-class athlete. Six-minute pace is fast running and puts you with the leaders in local races. Seven-minute pacers should finish in the top one-third in most races, eight-minute runners in the middle third, and nine-minute and slower ones in the back third. However, don't think you have lost if you don't compare well with the whole field. The real race is with your own pace.

**Second, compare the time with your other times at this**

**distance.** Overall times gain meaning as you run standard distances like the mile, 10 miles, and the marathon again and again—or as you run the same course repeatedly. You set personal records (PRs). You remember them, break them, or know exactly how far you miss them.

The place to store these records is in a diary. Lined up on two full shelves of my office are fat notebooks labeled "1978," "1977," and so on, all the way back to "1959." I'm prouder of them than of anything I've published, because these diaries are evidence of everywhere I've been. They tell my real story, not the one I edit for publishing in books like this one.

Everyone who runs needs such a diary. At the least, you have a place to brag and complain without boring anyone else. At best, you teach yourself about yourself. This makes it the most important book you'll ever see.

Write down all of your running records, no matter how insignificant they seem now. You never know the kind of story they might tell someday.

**Third, compare the time with your times from other events.** You might enter a 10,000-meter race this week, a marathon two weeks from now, and a 15-miler after that. Rarely will you try the same distance more than once or twice a year. So how do you compare the 10-kilometer, 15-mile, and marathon results? There are three ways: paces, scores, and grades.

I've told you how to figure pace. Decide if the slowdown or speedup in pace from race to race is what you'd expect as the distances get longer or shorter.

Scoring tables give point values to times for different races, taking into account expected changes in pace with distance. The Gerry Purdy Tables, for instance, give equal weight of 300 points to a 40-minute time (6:27 per mile pace) for 10 kilometers, 1:43 (6:52 pace) for 15 miles, and a 3:12 (7:20 pace) for the marathon. These tables appear in the Appendix at the back of the book.

I grade my everyday running as schools grade students, A-F. This system of combining times with feelings adapts well to races at all distances. Grade them this way:

*A* = super. Broke a PR for the distance or ran much farther/ faster than expected.

$B$ = good. Held a faster-than-normal pace all the way.

$C$ = fair. Pace was disappointing, but ran the whole way.

$D$ = poor. Hurting and forced to "survival shuffle" or walk to finish.

$F$ = awful. Dropped out.

If you want, you can make two more comparisons against other runners—both in this race and all races like it. These two are described in the sections that follow.

**Compare yourself with everyone else who ran here.** You probably got a place right after getting a time. An official may have stuck a numbered stick or card into your hand. If not, wait until everyone finishes, and then ask how you placed. Ask, too, how many runners started. (Nonfinishers are charged with a loss by default. You beat everyone who doesn't make the distance, so you often get to say you outran top-class runners simply because you went farther. I have beaten Olympians this way.)

With these numbers, figure how you ranked in the field. Divide the place by the number of starters to get a percentage rating. If, for example, you were ninety-eighth among 609, this ranks you in the top 16 percent. Next time, you might rank two hundredth of 2,000. The place will be lower, but the rating of 10 percent will be better. This system lets you compare accurately the finishes in different-sized races.

**Compare yourself with others of your age and sex.** Most short-distance races separate old runners from young and men from women. So in track and cross-country events, everyone usually starts together, but in the end results are split into divisions. These compensate for inequalities of age and sex.

See how you rank beside runners in your group at this race. Then, go to the tables in the Appendix and find out how your time compares to similar runners everywhere. The Purdy Tables give scores for both men and women, so that males must run faster for equal points. They show that if a woman and a man both run five-minute miles, she gets 700 points while he earns only about 350.

Ken Young worked up tables to grade runners by age. He figured that they peaked in their mid-20s and slow down gradually the further they are on either side of that age. A marathon time of three hours by a runner in his twenties earns about the same score as a 3:30 by a fifteen-year-old or a fifty-year-old.

In one of these comparisons, you're certain to find one or more ways that you won—or at least learn for sure how badly you lost.

### Self-Test 13
### What Does it All Mean?

1.  What was the distance of this race? (If metric, convert to miles and tenths.)

2.  What was your time? (List in minutes and tenths of minutes; six seconds is a tenth of a minute.)

3.  What was your pace per mile? (Divide race time by distance; convert the result back into minutes and seconds.)

4.  How much faster (or slower) was this pace than your normal training pace for a similar distance?

5.  What is your personal record for this distance? Or what was the old one if you broke it here?

6.  What was your point score for this race? (See the Purdy Tables in the Appendix.)

7.  What grade do you give yourself for this race? (See the grading standards in this chapter.)

8.  How did you rank in the overall field here? (Divide your place by the number of starters to find a percentage.)

9.  How did you rank in your division here? (Divide your place by the number of starters in your age or sex division to find a percentage.)

10. How did you score for your age-group? (See the Ken Young Age-Graded Tables in the Appendix.)

Note: Compare these results now with your times and places in previous races and later on in races yet to come.

# 14

## You Can Talk About It Now

No sooner is the race over than the instant replays begin. Runners talk so much after races that someone who doesn't run was moved to comment that running develops one set of muscles to an incredible level—those working the mouth.

We talk before races, too, but the purpose and tone then are much different. A worried mind and the manners of racing won't let us tell another racer, "I'm feeling great, and I'm going to burn up this course so badly they'll have to call the fire department to put it out." Your troubled mind tells you to be cautious, and to set up excuses in advance in case something goes wrong. Good manners demand that you be modest; never make aggressive noises that anyone else in the race might hear. So a typical prerace conversation goes like this:

"Hi, Jim."

"Oh, hello, Fred. How's it going?"

"Not so good. How about you?"

(Each tries to get the other to commit himself first.)

"Awful. Did I see you limping in the warmup?"

"Yeah. You sound like you have a cold."

"Yeah. What about your limp?"

"Oh, my knee's been giving me some trouble. What about your cold?"

"I caught it last week. It's got me down. How's your training been?"

"Terrible. I'm way down in my mileage. How's yours?"

"I'm barely running. I'm just doing this for a workout today."

"Same here. See you. Good luck."

"Sure, good luck. So long."

They fight each other to see who can dig a lower profile. They sound like two beginning runners on their way to the hospital. Five minutes later, they're on their way to the races of their lives.

Before races, we runners downgrade ourselves. Afterward, we gloat and exaggerate. We've earned the right to tell our equivalent of fish stories. Another conversation:

"Hi, Pete. How'd the race go?"

"Great, John. Just super. I broke three hours again. I'm going under regularly now."

(He did 2:59:30 and a year earlier had run 2:58:55, his only other sub-three-hour race.)

"How about you, Pete? Did you have a good one?"

"Sure did. I peaked for this race. Been doing 100-plus miles a week."

(If he took the best seven training days of his life, they'd total 101 miles.)

As we talk, we rerun each detail of the race, caressing and magnifying it with each telling. The miles grow longer, the hills higher, the wind stronger, the temperature hotter. The talk is as much a part of the race as training for it and pushing through it. Sharing experiences with people who have seen and felt the same things gives the race a final stamp of meaning.

Before he finished fourth in the Olympic Marathon, before he became even better known for his writing in *Sports Illustrated,* Kenny Moore wrote an article for his college alumni magazine. It explains better than anything I've read why runners talk so much.

> Human beings are reluctant to accept meaningless suffering. Families of dead soldiers refuse to believe such sacrifice could be in vain. In that way, the pain in a marathon's closing stages can be so great as to *force* meaning upon the run. Men submit to the ordeal not in spite of the pain but because of it. Competitive urges can carry you for 10 or 15 miles, but then the distance and discomfort already endured scream that this must not be for nothing. So you go on.
> Afterward, men hang stiffly on one another, too exhausted to untie their shoes . . . and jabber uncontrollably. The pain has made everything suffered so extraordinarily important that it *has* to be expressed. The cramp which seized your left leg coming off the hills

at 10 miles must be described in loving, urgent detail if only to the wall because nobody listens.

Later, when you recover, you remember your babbling and the others', and in an embarrassed sort of recognition you understand you shared something. It is the same for everyone.

It's the same everywhere people run long distances. The postrace scene is part family picnic, part happy hour at the corner bar, and part New Year's Eve. A common element to all of these is alcohol. Thirsty runners also drink plenty of beer, but it isn't the main fuel for our talk. We're drunk on the pain and fatigue we've just felt, on relief that it is over, and on pride that we've endured it.

Listen again to Kenny Moore:

> Perhaps when one stops, when one comes to accept that this is merely the way pain works on the mind, that there is no inherent meaning in repeating this sort of suffering, one will have died a little.
>
> The enduring satisfaction of distance running is not in records that will inevitably be broken, not in knowing that you were the best (read: "luckiest") on a given day. It lies in knowing that you have learned how to be brave and to do something better than you first thought you could, and perhaps in knowing that you amazed a few people along the way.

If we race to show ourselves we can be brave, we talk about it to amaze and be amazed by others.

The party lasts quite a while, and the same stories get told over and over. So no one will miss you and you won't miss anything if you get there a little late. Delay your talking while you take care of yourself for a few minutes. Otherwise, you'll delay your recovery by several days.

Recovery starts or stalls immediately after you finish, depending on how you treat yourself right away. If you stop two steps past the line, stagger to the nearest grassy spot and lie there uncovered for a half-hour, you recover slowly. The next few days' runs feel like they've been added onto the end of the race—or worse. But if you keep moving, cool slowly, and stretch, the damage done by the race is flushed out sooner.

Tom Osler has run more than 750 races lasting as long as twenty-four hours. In his *Serious Runner's Handbook* (World Publications, 1978), he gives this advice on postrace activity:

It is important to keep warm and to cool down gradually. Immediately put on warm clothes, then begin slow jogging and brisk walking. This should continue for 10-15 minutes before stopping. By keeping the circulation rapid, you help the body remove the waste products of fatigue. If it is cold, get inside as soon as you have completed the cooldown. Don't stand in the cool air and talk.

The postrace air cools instantly by 20 degrees, no matter what the temperature. It cools simply by stopping running. That's why you need to put on more clothes than you wore to race. Put on a dry T-shirt even if the day is warm, a full sweat suit if it's cool, and mittens and a cap if it's cold. Resist the temptation to strip next to naked or jump right into a pool in warm weather, or to go right inside from the cold to a hot shower. Either can make you sick.

I once raced 10 miles on a 90-degree day. A few minutes after finishing, I wore only shorts and shoes as I sped home on my motorbike. The cool breeze was delightful, but the head cold I caught two days later wasn't so pleasant. Another time, I raced outdoors in subzero weather and ended with frostbite on the tips of my ears. I went straight from the course to the shower. Two days later, I had a chest cold.

Racing is shock enough for the body without subjecting your body to drastic temperature changes right afterward. Your reserves to fight off illness are already low. You don't need much extra jolt for a cold or the flu to move in. This might happen if you don't cool off gradually.

Something else is guaranteed if you don't keep moving. Your overworked muscles, saturated with fatigue wastes, stiffen quickly if you stop suddenly. They have less trouble if you let them slow down by degrees. Don't sit down. Walk until you can run very slowly again. If you can't run continuously, alternate short runs and walks. Do this for 5 to 10 minutes. Walk only for another 5 to 10 minutes. Finish with a few minutes of stretching exercises.

If you can wait a few more minutes before joining the party, take a shower. If not, go ahead and talk. Don't miss the talking now. If these people don't listen to your stories, no one will.

## Self-Test 14
## How Do You Explain Yourself?

1. Do you feel proud that you were brave enough to put up with the fatigue and pain, and relieved that it's over?

2. Do you have stories of the race that *must* be shared with anyone who will listen?

3. Do you want to grab people who normally would remain strangers and talk to them about what you've done?

4. Do you ask others about their races as a way of getting them to ask you about yours?

5. Do you have the urge to exaggerate (time, distance, difficulty, ease, etc.)?

6. Does your mouth run loose the way it does when you've had a little too much to drink?

7. Do you feel embarrassed when you think back later on how you babbled after the race?

8. Did you take a few minutes away from the party to do things that would make you recover better for the next few days?

9. Did you stay on your feet, and change into warmer and drier clothes?

10. Did you take a proper cooldown, including some gentle running, some walking, and some stretching for at least 10 to 15 minutes?

Note: These are all "yes" questions.

# 15

## It Can't Help but Hurt

Hard racing can't help but hurt. I've said this before, and I'll say it again before the book ends. I say it in this chapter not only so you'll expect pain as an inevitable by-product of racing, but so you'll know that all pains aren't bad. Some are good and others indifferent.

I want you to learn here and in the next two chapters how to differentiate between various types of pain—to be proud of handling the good, to run through the indifferent, and to spot the bad and know how to keep it from getting worse.

Like the poor, the sore runner will always be with us. No matter how much money you make, if you spend that much and more, you're poor. By that standard, I've always been poor, because several things conspire to keep me in poverty while I earn scandalous amounts of money:

- Material wants quickly and automatically expand to gobble up available cash.

- The temptation is too strong to spend what I have now, instead of squirreling it away in the bank for a dry spell later on.

- Credit cards are even more tempting. They shout, "Spend! Spend!" with money that isn't there. Instead of saving for the rainy days, I get the American Express, Visa, and other bills on those days.

- Then, instead of cutting back on my spending and increasing my savings, I shift the blame to my creditors and accuse them of demanding too much of my hard-earned pay.

Injury is any pain or set of pains that keeps a runner from doing all the running he wants. And by that standard, I've always been injured. Despite my quite relaxed approach by the standards of the sport, I've always raced to my limits and wanted to go beyond. My wishes for speed and distance expand to meet the available resources. In other words, I run faster and longer until I find my breaking point. This is a shifting thing. Sometimes, it is 30 miles a week at eight minutes apiece. Other times, it has been twice that far and two minutes per mile faster. The constant is that I'm always being drawn toward physical bankruptcy.

It's no easier to put running in the bank (to save energy and enthusiasm for another day) than it is to put money away. The attitude I share with most runners is, "If you have it, spend it." I race or run 15 miles or so on many Saturdays, spending everything I have. Then, I can barely move for the next two or three days. If I were wiser about conserving my natural resources, I would spread the effort more evenly over those three or four days, and end up accomplishing more with less stress.

Spending what isn't there—the "credit-card syndrome"—is even worse economics. I'm no marathoner. A marathon is a long, hard run, requiring great background mileage and patience. I have neither, yet I run a marathon or two each year. I run on credit. I realize it's going to put me deeply in debt. But I say to myself, "I don't have to worry about that until the bill comes due later."

Then, when I've bankrupted myself physically and get hurt, I act as if someone is picking on me. "The gods are against me," I say. "Every time I start to get in good shape, something like this happens."

Training theorists, running shoemakers, and sports doctors all have taken commendable—in some cases even revolutionary— strides forward in injury-prevention techniques. Yet they haven't been able to stay ahead of us runners who insist on hurting ourselves in about the same ways and at about the same rates as always. Runners may be getting hurt now at six minutes per mile instead of eight. They may be hurting themselves at 50 miles per week instead of 25. But about two in three of them still get hurt badly enough to slow down or stop.

This 60-70 percent casualty rate comes from *Runner's World* surveys, and it may be a low estimate. It doesn't include the "running wounded" who won't stop to let themselves heal. And it includes only those who have recovered or have enough faith in their recovery powers that they are still reading a running magazine. It doesn't account for the thousands of people who drop out of the sport each year because they don't know how to deal with chronic injuries.

This is part of an all-or-nothing mentality many runners and most racers have. There are no in-betweens for us. Either we work through pain or get completely away from it. Runners face this decision every day, because in the same person lives both a hypochondriac and a masochist. The hypochondriac worries that pain will keep him from running. He dwells on it, fears it, and curses it. His mind magnifies minor aches into major ones. The masochist, on the other hand, wallows in his pain. He courts it, welcomes it, and challenges it. And after he has been through it, he brags about how well he suffered.

To understand how a runner can have such different views of pain, you have to realize that there are different kinds of pain —good, bad and indifferent. Good pains are the natural and temporary results of honest effort. They are the "rigor mortis" that sets in during a fast mile, and the numbing weariness of the last miles of a marathon. They result from the strain of interval work and the fatigue of a long, steady run. Meeting and getting through these pains is one reason to run.

Bad pains lead to runners' hypochondria. Bad pains stand in the way of normal running. They are tears of muscles, tendons, cartilages, and ligaments, or breaks in the bones. They are feared because they can't be "run through."

Indifferent pains are the rather harmless by-products of running—such things as blisters, mild muscle soreness, and stiffness. They are neither pleasant nor limiting, so they are ignored.

Whether the pains are good, bad, or indifferent, we runners have always had them and always will. This is our nature and the nature of our sport.

The committed runner is like an impatient driver on a freeway. The speed limit signs read 55, but you confuse their meaning. You forget that the limit is posted for your safety, not to hold you back arbitrarily. You never drive below the limit, but always right at it or a little above. Pain in running is a speed limit, a safety warning. When you push beyond it, the body flashes a warning light saying "Danger Ahead!" As long as runners race at or past the physical limits, we'll get hurt. But if we didn't push our limits, we wouldn't be racers.

Racing is an occasional challenge that makes the rest of what I do seem easier and better. If I ran easily all the time, always for the same short distances, after a while the "easy" would seem hard and the "short" would feel long. That's what happens when there's nothing to compare it with. This is why I vary my distances and add some runs about twice as long as the others. This is why I throw in a few brief accelerations each day. Above all, this is why I run a race once a month. These things accent my everyday running, making me more aware of how nice it is.

Feeling uncomfortable once in a while makes the days of comfort more pleasant. That's where the fun of running lies—on the other side of adversity. A little pain is more the spice of life than variety. A little bad is the seasoning that brings out the flavor of the good.

Food never tastes so good as after we've missed a meal or two. Water tastes best after we've run ourselves dry. A shower is most cleansing after we've worked up a dirty, smelly lather of sweat. Sleep is most satisfying after we've worn ourselves out. We take the greatest pride in our little acts of bravery after we've faced up to our fears.

A philosophy professor once told me, "Everyone needs a few minutes of pain in order to make the rest of the time more pleasurable. If the pain isn't a normal part of the day, one must contrive it."

### Self-Test 15
### What Are Your Symptoms?

1.   Did the thought of food nauseate you for a few hours after you finished? Then did you have a hard-to-satisfy appetite?

2. Was your weight two or more pounds below normal the day after the race as a result of dehydration?

3. Were you thirstier than usual for several days as you tried to make up for the fluid loss?

4. Did you urinate less often than usual, and was it a dark yellow from the wastes of hard effort?

5. Did you have trouble falling asleep the night after the race, and waking up the next several mornings?

6. Did the race leave you with any blisters, bruised toenails, or muscle cramps?

7. Were you sore the next day in the thigh muscles, just above the knees? In the hamstrings? In the calves or ankles?

8. Did the start of your run the next day feel like the twenty-seventh mile of a marathon?

9. All day the next day, did you feel like you had a hang-over? Were you heavy, clumsy, sluggish, and generally unenthusiastic about making any physical effort?

10. Did you feel even more stiff and tired the second day after the race?

Note: Answer these questions in the first two days after racing. I'd expect many "yes" answers, since all of these are normal reactions to racing.

# 16

## Clearing Away the Damage

If the few hours after the race are a time for acting drunk with pride, the next few days are when you feel the hangover. This is when you pay the tab for going past your everyday limits. The reason you feel bad is simple enough. In your excitement with the race, you dipped into an emergency fuel supply—your adrenaline. It made you go a minute per mile faster or twice as far as you usually can. But that wasn't a gift. You only borrowed it, and now you must pay it back.

You escaped injury. (If you did hurt yourself seriously enough to limp during or right after the race, go straight to chapter 17.) You have only the normal next-day pains, and they're bad enough. You feel like the Boston Marathon field trampled you in your sleep. As you try to wake up and get out of bed, you think your body is made of rusty steel wool. If the race was short and faster than you're used to running, your hamstring and calf muscles hurt; your throat and chest burn. If the race was longer or hillier than you normally run, you feel it in the thighs, hips, and ankles. Your feet are sore from blisters, blackened toenails, or just the pounding.

At first, you couldn't fall asleep, and now can't get enough sleep. Your appetite and thirst are extraordinary, yet your weight is down by several pounds. Pardon me for being indelicate, but this is important—you're constipated, and your urine is a frighteningly bright yellow. You move with all the grace and spunk of an eighty-year-old arthritic.

You may not have all of these symptoms at once. But you're sure to feel at least one of them after each race until you even-

94

tually experience them all. They aren't bad pains, but are friendly signs that you raced hard enough and now need time to recover.

Recovery seems to go backward at first. You feel worse the morning after the race than you did right after, and worse yet the second day. It takes that long for the "drunk" to wear off, and the soreness and fatigue to settle in completely. You typically hit bottom about forty-eight hours after racing. You aren't tempted to do much running in this state, and you aren't thinking much about racing again. After, another twenty-four to forty-eight hours pass, the worst of the hurts disappear. You think you're ready to start training for another race, but that's where you're wrong—perhaps dangerously wrong. Recovery isn't finished when your legs loosen up; it has only begun.

Racing tears you down in more ways than one. I see at least three stages of recovery. As well as my unscientific mind can define them, they are: (1) muscular, (2) chemical, and (3) psychological. Recovery from muscle soreness and fatigue comes quickest. Even marathoners get over it within a few days. But it takes longer to restore body chemistry to its normal balance, and still longer to forget how bad this race felt so you can start looking forward to the next one. The whole recovery process is seldom complete in less than a week. It sometimes takes a month or more.

This may sound like too long. I once thought so, too. Like most runners, I figured I'd recovered from one weekend to the next, and I raced almost every weekend. However, one year I couldn't race as often because I worked at least two weekends a month. That was 1968. I wrote of it in *Run Gently, Run Long*:

"Ah, 1968! I didn't know why, and it wasn't planned that way, but everything was right in my running then. I had two speeds—easy and all-out—and apparently had stumbled onto the right balance between the two. In 1968, I ran my best times at everything from one mile to 18-plus miles. I was healthy and fast without knowing why."

I now know why. It had to do with the amount of racing I did. But because I'd found the right amount accidentally and didn't know what it was, I drifted away from it after that year.

Before I tell the bad news, let me relate the good. In the last eight months of 1968, I set 15 personal records. I never had the slightest injury or illness. I trained modestly, averaging a gentle fifty minutes a day with no fast running outside of races. Most significantly, I averaged 5 percent of my total running as races each month in that period. (The lowest was 2 percent, the highest 10 percent.)

Then, my weekends opened up again. Nothing changed in the way I ran except my racing. The quantity of races became more important than the quality. In the next months, despite all my racing, I set only one PR. I was hurt or ill often, and nearly always tired. The racing percentages show why.

In 21 of the 30 months, I raced more than 10 percent of my running. Seven months topped 20 percent. I peaked at 45 percent. A 23 percent month put me in the hospital for a foot operation and finally got me thinking about the right balance between gentle runs and races.

If I wanted to run well, I had to race regularly. If percentages fell below 2 percent, I didn't have a racing edge; I felt clumsy at the faster tempo. But that was rarely a problem. My usual mistake was racing too much, not too little. Too much for me was more than 10 percent, which didn't allow me enough time between races to recover and rebuild. My performances suffered first, and then my body did.

Five percent racing—one minute or one mile in every 20— seems about ideal. I tried to say that in past books, but the math got cumbersome. Now, I've simplified the formula for recovery time. I borrow it from two of the sport's best minds.

Jack Foster is a 2:11 marathoner from New Zealand. If 2:11 doesn't mean much to you, think of it as 26 straight five-minute miles. If that still doesn't impress you, consider that Foster was forty-one years old when he ran it, and that he didn't begin running until he was thirty-two. Jack writes in *Tale of the Ancient Marathoner,* "My method is roughly to have a day off for every mile I've raced. If I've run a hard 26-mile road race, then I don't like to race again for at least 26 days. I'll go for daily runs, okay, but no really hard effort."

Training the amounts Foster does, his racing under this formula works out to less than 10 percent. We who run less probably need an extra day for each mile of the race. That's what Tom Osler recommends in *Serious Runner's Handbook.* Osler says, "As a rule of thumb, for the well-trained runner it takes about one day for each mile of the race for complete recovery. . . . The runner will require longer periods if he is not thoroughly trained. . . . I believe [he] should *double* the above-mentioned recovery time before he attempts another all-out performance. This means that he should wait 10 days after a five-mile race, 20 days after a 10-miler and two months after a marathon."

### Table 3
### Spaces Between Races

| Racing Distance | Recovery | Rebuilding | Total Time |
|---|---|---|---|
| mile or 1,500 m. | 2 days | 5 days | 1 week* |
| 2 miles or 3,000 m. | 2 days | 5 days | 1 week* |
| 3 miles or 5,000 m. | 3 days | 4 days | 1 week* |
| 6 miles or 10,000 m. | 1 week | 1 week | 2 weeks |
| 10 miles or 15,000 m. | 1½ weeks | 1½ weeks | 3 weeks |
| half-marathon or 20,000 m. | 2 weeks | 2 weeks | 4 weeks |
| 15 miles or 15,000 m. | 2½ weeks | 2½ weeks | 5 weeks |
| 20 miles or 30,000 m. | 3 weeks | 3 weeks | 6 weeks |
| marathon | 4 weeks | 4 weeks | 8 weeks |

* Allow a minimum of one week between even the shortest races.

Note: These periods are based on one day of recovery and one day of rebuilding for each mile of an all-out race. During recovery, take no extra-long or hard training, no increase in training amounts, and no races (even casual ones). During rebuilding, train normally and possibly increase the amount, but don't race seriously.

I suggest a "one-and-one" system—one day for each mile of the race to recover, and one more day per mile to rebuild or replace lost training. For convenience, let's say your race was seven miles. That means you spend one week recovering. Do only easy maintenance running of perhaps 30 to 45 minutes a day. Try nothing long, hard or fast, but keep running. We seem to recover quicker with light running than with total rest. In the rebuilding period (the second week after a seven-mile race), resume normal training. Return longer and harder runs, and some speed to your schedule—but *don't race*! If you get lured into a race, treat it as a workout and don't go all-out.

You owe yourself all of this time to clear away the damage done by a race. If you keep tearing down faster than you repair, the good and indifferent pains of racing eventually turn into the bad kind that stop you.

### Self-Test 16
### How Long Does it Take?

1. What was the distance of the race? (In miles; convert from meters if necessary.)

2. How many days of recovery should you allow after the race? (One day per mile of racing.)

3. What was your typical short, easy run for recovery from longer ones as you trained for this race?

4. Have you scheduled anything but similar short, easy runs for the race-recovery period? (The right answer is "no." Certainly don't try to go more than double the time or distance listed in question 3.)

5. How many days of rebuilding should you allow after you've recovered? (An additional one day per mile of racing.)

6. As rebuilding begins, are you ready and eager to go back to normal training, including long runs? (If you don't say "yes," recover some more or read chapter 17.)

7. Have you scheduled any races during the rebuilding period? (Please say "no," unless the event is low-key and treated only as a part of training.)

8. What is the total number of days set aside for recovery and rebuilding? (Add answers to questions 2 and 5.)

9. If you're interested in a more exact figure on minimum recovery-rebuilding, how much running do you need between races to get a 10 percent racing ratio? (Multiply the time or distance of the race by 10, then run that much before racing again.)

10. For ideal recovery-rebuilding, how much running do you need between races to get a 5 percent racing ratio? (Multiply the race time or distance by 20, then run that much before racing again.)

# 17

## Coming Back from Injuries

Ted Haydon numbers me among his thousands of converts. In 1960, he introduced me to the idea that racing is too good to stop when the school track season ends. He offered then, and still does, a year-round program through the University of Chicago Track Club.

Haydon is now recognized as one of the country's finest coaches. He also is credited with one of sports medicine's truest statements. When asked why runners get hurt so often, Ted referred to an old gospel song. He said the foot bone's connected to the ankle bone, the ankle bone's connected to the shin bone, and so on. But the problem is, none of these is connected to the head bone.

This is most true when we race. We put the most strain on our feet and legs at a time when our heads are somewhere else. My experience has proved Haydon right dozens of times since 1960—almost always as a direct or indirect result of racing. If there's one area of running where my experience is unsurpassed, it's in getting hurt.

I won't say you'll never hurt yourself. Risk of injury is part of racing. All I can do here is to help you recognize if a pain is an injury instead of a normal part of racing. Then I can suggest ways to get over it quickly, so you can risk another injury in the next race.

I limit this chapter to race-inflicted injuries. You know you have one if it hurts early or late. If you first feel pain during the race and it remains after you stop, it's likely to be a true injury. Normal stiffness doesn't set in until later. On the other hand, this soreness should go away in a few days. If you still hurt a week after racing, you're probably injured.

To treat yourself, first remove the mystique and the mumbo-jumbo language from running medicine, and get rid of the notion that you can do nothing to help yourself. You don't have to be a doctor, or know the names of the bones, muscles, and tendons, or know the physiological principles behind the injury to practice effective first aid and to keep the same thing from happening again.

This self-help plan tells what you can do without going to a doctor, spending a lot of money, or losing too much running time. Start with the simplest cures, and work by steps toward the most complicated. Chances are you'll be healed before you get to the bottom of the list.

A saying among doctors is, "If you hear hoofbeats, think first of horses, not zebras." This means that when doing their diagnostic detective work, they should start with the obvious sources of the problem and work toward the exotic ones. Look first at your obvious information, the most obvious being that you once were healthy and now you're hurt. You want to find the cause of the pain and eliminate it.

Doctors who don't know running are likely to tell you, "If it hurts to run, then stop running. That'll be $20." They're half-right. You should stop doing the kind of running that's causing the pain. But rarely do you need to stop all running—or to visit doctors. If you take care of little "horses," you may never need to worry about "zebras" with big names and complex treatments.

### 1. How Much Does it Hurt?

When you first hurt, find out how serious the pain is by testing what you can and cannot do. Define the degree of pain by how much it limits motions or changes your running form.

**First degree.** While there is no limitation of motion, there is low-grade pain at the start of training, decreasing as the run progresses, then reappearing after you stop.

**Second degree.** Pain remains constant or increases as runs continue, but with little effect on running form.

**Third degree.** You detect mild pain on easy runs, and severe pain with disturbance of form on hard ones.

**Fourth degree.** It is impossible to run without great pain and a pronounced limp.

Recognize that pain is a voice inside you to remind you that you're pushing yourself too far. Treat pain as a friendly warning that you've crossed the boundary between training and straining.

And heed the words of Dr. Richard Schuster, a noted podiatrist, who says, "Runners should tolerate a little bit of annoyance but no more than that. I think it's a crazy habit some of our runners have, running through pain. I think you should try to run through annoyance, but don't run through pain. Pain is destruction."

## 2. What Do You Do First?

Put aside your old training schedule and stopwatch for now, because they probably put you in the bad shape you're in. Ignore your usual training partners, because you'll either feel depressed about not being able to keep up with them, or you'll forget yourself, keep up, and do further damage.

Tune in completely to your level of pain and the effect it is having on your running form.

**First degree.** No dramatic changes in routine are required, other than a more thorough warmup. Get rid of the pain before trying anything hard.

**Second degree.** Eliminate the runs that cause pain to increase. These usually include races, hard speedwork, and the longest training runs.

**Third degree.** Use run-walk "intervals." Start very slowly and cautiously. When pain builds to a form-disturbing level, walk and perhaps do some stretching exercises. Run again, walk, run, walk, etc.

**Fourth degree.** Substitute a related activity that causes no pain, such as walking, bicycling, or swimming. Do it in amounts about equal to your normal running. According to Dr. Kenneth Cooper, 2½ miles of walking, 5 miles of bicycling, and a quarter-mile of swimming provide about the same benefits as a mile of running.

Work gradually toward lighter degrees of pain—fourth to third degree, third to second, etc. Do some careful testing once each week to see if you're ready to advance. If you had fourth-degree pain, try some run-walk intervals. If your pain was second-degree, cautiously try a longer or faster run.

### 3. Why Did it Happen?

Nearly all running injuries are self-inflicted. They don't happen by accident, but usually are the result of going too long, too fast, or a combination of the two.

Once you've recovered enough to go back to your old schedule, examine that schedule. Determine the stress load it imposes in an attempt to prevent the injury from happening again.

Ask yourself the following questions.

**How much do I run?** Surveys in *Runner's World* indicate that 50-mile-a-week runners are nearly twice as likely to be injured as those who run 25 miles a week. Those who jump suddenly from 25 to 50 miles are prime injury candidates.

**How fast do I run?** Those who race are about twice as likely to get hurt as nonracers, both because of the stresses of the race and the intense training to prepare for it.

**How often do I run?** Everyday runners are injured more often than those who take days off during the week. Chronic fatigue leads to injuries.

Based on your answers, make permanent adjustments in your training routine if you see obvious weaknesses. Increase training mileages and paces only gradually, and allow break-in periods when shifting from flats to hills, soft surfaces to roads, training shoes to racing spikes, etc. Mileage, for instance, probably should not climb by more than 10 percent a week.

Speed builds strength, but it also can kill. Allow plenty of recovery time after speed work and races, and don't make a habit of running fast when you're either sore or tired from the previous day's session.

Make rest and recovery days a regular part of your program. Bill Bowerman, developer of the "hard-easy" system, says few runners can work hard more than three days a week. Spread these days out over the full week, and relax between them.

## 4. How Do You Start?

When you're eager to get into a run, warming-up exercises seem to stand in the way. But this part of the session becomes more important than ever once you've been injured.

Adopt a warmup routine that includes the following features.

**Start with stretching and strengthening exercises.** Pay special attention to the weak area where you were injured.

**Tiptoe into the run.** There's no way of judging how a run is going to feel before it starts. You may hurt terribly on days when you thought you'd made a miracle recovery overnight, and you may loosen up completely after a crippled start. Therefore, you must learn to withhold judgement on a run until it is 10-15 minutes old. It takes that long for the pattern of the day to announce itself.

Always start, no matter how badly you think the run might go. But beyond simply vowing to start, have only the loosest plan for that day, subject to change after 10 or 15 minutes.

Begin at a slow, careful, running-on-eggs shuffle. Let the kinks work themselves out without putting any strain on them. Let the day's pace find itself in the first mile or two. At that point, assess the way you feel, and make an honest decision about the run based on those feelings. Be prepared to go faster and farther than planned, to run as planned, to cut back, or even to abort.

**Stop and stretch.** Running tightens the leg muscles, and the tightness may produce pain. Mid-run stretching breaks can reverse this. A convenient, not-too-conspicuous, all-purpose exercise is the "Rodgers stretch," named for Bill Rodgers, who stopped to tie his shoes several times in the 1975 Boston Marathon. The exercise resembles shoe-tying. Put one foot behind the other as if you're starting a sprint; then straighten the back leg, trying to stretch its heel to the ground. Repeat with the other leg.

## 5. When Do You Run?

If you've been hurt, don't get the day off to a running start. Soreness usually is at its peak when you get up. You feel, as Rocky Balboa did, that you need to call a taxi to take you from the bedroom to the bathroom.

Dr. Richard Schuster says, "People who run in the morning are more apt to get hurt than those who run later in the day. They are physically cold and stiff in the morning. They want to get the day going, so they don't take time to warm up. But it's important for these people to warm up more than they ordinarily would."

If you insist on running early, warm up more and start slower than you normally would. If possible, be out of bed, moving around for an hour before running. This gets much of the sleep from your head, and the stiffness and soreness from your body.

## 6. Where Do You Run?

Conventional wisdom is that hard surfaces are bad and soft ones are good. Most runners assume that injuries happen because we pound ourselves too much. Hard surfaces do give us a pounding. But this, in most cases, leads only to temporary discomfort, not to injury or the aggravation of injury. Surprisingly, *Runner's World* surveys show no significant difference in injury rates between those who run on hard and soft surfaces.

If I'm injured, I *prefer* to run on a hard surface—not because I enjoy the pounding but because I like the smoothness. Hard surfaces like roads are almost always smooth.

Soft running places like grass produce less shock, but the trade-off is that they are uneven. The feet constantly are twisting to compensate for it, and the heels sink in more than normal. So the legs get an extra up-and-down and side-to-side workout that they don't need if they're prone to injury.

I've suspected this for a long time, but now I have no less an authority than Dr. Schuster to back me up. He says, "Running on a smooth dirt road would be best. Paths are full of holes. Grass is bad because it hides the irregularities."

Hills can be an injury-producer, too. The three main areas of injury are knees, Achilles tendons, and shins. Uphill running puts extra stretch and strain on the Achilles. Downhills multiply the shock to knees and shins.

### 7. What Do You Wear?

I share a dream with all runners who have ever had sore feet and legs. (This is to say all runners. A runner who has never been sore from the toenails to the knees is as rare as a skier who has never had a cold nose.)

The dream is that someday, somewhere, somehow we'll find the perfect shoe. It will make the foot feel like it is swaddled in a protective cocoon, which transmits no shock, gives no irritation, and yet is as flexible as being barefoot. The more a runner hurts, the more he chases this dream— from one shoestore to the next. The promise of perfection in the next model is what keeps more than a dozen running-shoemakers in business.

Sore runners are brand-jumpers. Manufacturers can't count on our loyalty, because as soon as we find that one shoe doesn't do what we thought it should, we switch. We keep switching, because no shoe can be as perfect as we want it.

Any shoes, no matter how well made, start breaking down after their first few hundred miles. Recently, my Achilles tendons grew tender. I'd been reluctant to give up my favorite shoes, and the heels were worn beyond the critical quarter-inch that produces imbalances. The middle layer of rubber had compressed, losing much of its original height. The plastic in the heel counter was cracked. As soon as I traded in the shoes for new ones, the pain disappeared.

The points here are: first, buy the best shoes for your needs, and second, throw them away before they hurt you.

Shoe modifications might help, too. Dr. Schuster recommends heel lifts as a preventive measure for many injuries. Heel lifts relieve pressure on the backs of the legs, which often are tight in runners. Other running doctors prescribe heel wedges to reduce side-to-side motion. Arch supports help control excessive motion of the forefoot.

### 8. What Can You Take?

Whenever a runner is hurt enough that he can't run normally, he is prey to all sort of missionaries and salesmen. He wants a quick cure, and is willing to change lifelong habits or to pay dearly for it. The longer he stays hurt, the more of a straw-grabber he becomes, and salesmen have him in their pocket.

Runners generally are not drug-takers. We may even resist taking aspirin. But when we're hurt, we may gobble aspirin to reduce inflammation and pain.

A *Runner's World* reader commented, "I've discovered that two aspirin taken about an hour before a run does more for me than three visits to a podiatrist. Namely, it allows me to run pain-free."

Dr. George Sheehan answered, "I see no reason why you shouldn't do it."

You may have previously taken perverse pleasure in flaunt-ing your vitamin J (junkfood) habit. But suddenly you find yourself looking into vegetarian and natural-food diets and exotic supplements in hopes of finding a quick cure.

You hear that Achilles tendinitis is related to high uric acid levels, which are related to eating lots of rich, meaty foods. Maybe if you cut out meat . . .

But you still need plenty of protein to repair the tissues being pounded during your runs. You read of protein supple-ments. Maybe if you started taking a few of those . . .

A doctor in southern California says he's found a direct correlation between deterioration of the tendons and clogging of the arteries. Maybe you need to go on a strict low-cholesterol diet . . .

If none of this works, maybe you should see a doctor for a cortisone shot. Or maybe you should consider tendon-lengthen-ing surgery . . .

Whoa! Your imagination is running away. You are hearing the hoofbeats of zebras and setting out on a wild chase after them. There are plenty of horses to track down first, and they're much easier to catch.

### Self-Test 17
### How Do You Heal Yourself?

- Where do you hurt? (Just name the area; it isn't necessary to make an exact diagnosis of the injury.)

- Have you been hurt this way before? (If so, review the cause, symptoms, treatment, and duration for clues on what to do—or not to do—this time.)

- When did it start hurting this time? (If you felt it during or right after a race or hard run, it is abnormal.)

- Does it still hurt after the normal pains of hard work should have disappeared? (Normal stiffness should go away in less than a week.)

* * * * * *

1.  What is the degree of pain? (First, second, third, or fourth; see descriptions in the text.)

2.  Have you adjusted your training to fit the degree of pain? (If not, see the advice in this chapter.)

3.  Have you figured out what caused the injury? (If not, see the text for possible explanations.)

4.  Have you adjusted your warmup routine to compensate for the injury? (If not, this chapter tells how.)

5.  Do you run first thing in the morning? (This is the worst time to run when you're injured.)

6.  Do you run on rough ground, hills, or both? (Smooth, flat surfaces are kindest to injured legs.)

7.  Have you checked or changed your shoes lately? (The shoes themselves, their wear patterns, or their inserts may cause or prevent injuries.)

8.  Have you taken anything by shot or by mouth to help the injury? (The answer should be "no" until you have exhausted the more conservative remedies in question 1-7.)

Note: The questions marked with bullets are covered in the introduction to this chapter. Others correspond to the numbered sections of the text.

# 18

# Coming Back for More (or Less)

"It takes all the running you can do," wrote Lewis Carroll in *Alice in Wonderland,* "to keep in the same place. If you want to go somewhere else, you must run at least twice as fast as that."

That may have been true for Alice's running, but it isn't necessarily so for the kind we do. We sometimes progress without going either twice as fast or twice as far. We move ahead while appearing to stay where we are or go backward.

There will be times in the remaining chapters of this book when I urge you to train faster and longer. This isn't one of those times. Here, I'm telling you how to race as well or better on the same amount of running, or even on less. You simply make what you do more efficient by correcting your mistakes.

This is a review chapter to remind you of principles from the first seventeen chapters that you may have ignored or forgotten. Now is the best time to learn or relearn them for two reasons. First, the recent race is still fresh in your mind; no matter how well you did there, you want to find ways to do better. Second, if you want to move up to faster and longer races, you need to solve basic problems before extra pace and distance compound them.

You have trained for the last race, tapered for it, run it, and recovered from it. You've gone through the full cycle at least once, so you aren't a novice anymore. Now, as you start a new cycle, you have a history of errors to learn and advance from, or to ignore and repeat. Review where you have been and what you have done there. See which of the following statements you have made. Find where you tried to cheat the principles of racing and have been caught. Then correct, refine, and improve—but don't add anything yet.

I list here the most common complaints of new racers, and their causes and cures.

**"I never had any zip when I was training. I seemed tired and sore most of the time."**

*Complaint:* You have chronic fatigue, often accompanied by low-grade muscle, tendon, and joint pain. The most damaging part of it, though, is its erosion of your enthusiasm. You don't look forward to running when you're tired all the time.

*Causes:* It could have one of three—or all three together. The first is too quick a buildup in average daily times or distances; the second, not enough (or any) easy days; and the third, going too long on your long runs.

*Cures:*

1. Add no more than 10 percent per run per week as you progress. This is just three minutes in a half-hour run, and even it may be too much.
2. Follow every long-hard run with at least one short-easy for recovery, and consider taking one day a week off in times of heavy stress.
3. Rarely go more than twice your average daily time or distance, and never more than triple.

*Review:* Chapters 3, 4, and 5 on training.

**"I felt really good until about a week before the race. Then, I took my longest run and it wiped me out."**

*Complaint:* You thought you could make one last push to cram in extra training. Instead of improving, you started the race already in the hole. You ran too hard, too late, and never fully recovered from it.

*Cause:* Training has a delayed reaction. The work you do this week doesn't make you better this week, but sometime later. It can set you back temporarily. This often happens in the last days before races, when runners worry that they haven't trained long enough. Races can't be won by late training, but they can be lost there.

*Cure:* Taper for important races. Starting a full week before the race, cut your training in half. Take no more long or hard runs. Possibly rest one or more days to be sure you start fresh.

*Review:* Chapters 7, 8, and 9 on the last days.

**"I was dashing all the way, trying desperately to hold a pace that seemed too fast."**

*Complaint:* You didn't have enough speed. The race pace was so much faster than you usually go that it made you feel awkward and out of breath. You labored from the start and never fell into a good running rhythm.

*Cause:* Speed was too new to you, and you weren't trained to handle it. Typical training runs were a minute to several minutes per mile slower than races. I don't say you should train faster all the time, but you need some speed training if you ever expect to race more comfortably.

*Cures:* There are two. The first is racing itself; it gets smoother the more regularly you do it. The second involves adding spurts of speed to otherwise gentle daily runs. Make each about 5 percent of your program by racing once every few weeks and spurting to race pace for one minute in every twenty of training. Racing still won't be easy, but it will be more familiar.

*Review:* Chapters 3, 4, and 5 on training, ànd chapter 16 on race frequency.

**"I thought I was holding a steady pace, but the last half of the race was 20 seconds per mile slower than the first."**

*Complaint:* Your pace was erratic. You tried to spread your effort evenly over the entire distance, but your split times show that you wound down as you went.

*Cause:* Good pacing goes against your instincts. You must pull back on your reins early when you feel like going fast, and then go to the whip later when you want to ease off. Steady-paced racing—the most efficient kind—doesn't feel even. The effort needed to hold it increases all the way.

*Cure:* Divide the distance into halves. Run the first half with the planned restraint of a scientist, and the last half with the creative abandon of an artist. Later, compare the times for the parts. They should be within five seconds per mile of each other. If they aren't, adjust the starting pace next time.

*Review:* Chapters 10, 11, and 13 on tactics, pacing, and times.

### "I handled the pace okay, but I ran out of gas near the end."

*Complaint:* The distance seemed too long, despite the fact that your training should have been adequate. You averaged more than the minimum one-third of the race per day that I recommend.

*Cause:* You may not have taken runs long enough—or enough long runs. I ask you to go twice your average time or distance once a week, and to add two more above-average runs weekly.

*Cure:* If you took long runs every other day and still had trouble, make them longer yet. I generally advise making the longest run 30 percent of the week's total, the other two long runs 20 percent and short runs 10 percent each, with one optional day (which usually means rest). But if you have distance problems, consider making the long runs longer, and all the other days easier or optional. Increase the longest runs to as much as 40 percent and the other two to 25-30 percent, while keeping the week's total the same.

*Review:* Chapters 3, 4, and 5 on training.

### "I'm disappointed. I have run faster than this in time-trials by myself."

*Complaint:* Your race results didn't even match those from training. Alone on your own measured courses you run without interference and get excellent times. Here, you wasted too much time dodging other people.

*Cause:* First, training routes almost always are shorter than you think, so they give faster times than accurately measured race courses. Second, you are leaving your best races on the neighborhood streets if you push your training that hard.

*Cure:* Save your racing for where it counts—at the race. There, your times and distances are accurate. In all but the most crowded races, the other runners help your time much more than they hurt it. If you race your training, it becomes straining, and no one can do that for long without breaking down. Avoid the urge to race it by training for distances without timing them, or by running for periods of time without knowing how far you go. Don't combine the two factors of distance and time.

*Review:* Chapters 3, 4, and 5 on training, and chapter 16 on racing frequency.

**"The race has been over for a week now, but I'm still just running through the motions."**

*Complaint:* You don't think you're recovering fast enough. The aching tiredness in your legs is gone, but you still don't feel right. You wonder if you'll be ready to race again this weekend.

*Cause:* All-out racing—the only kind I talk about in this book—is a shock. It hurts on several levels, and you must recover from each before you shock yourself again. The levels are muscular, chemical, and psychological. Each is deeper than the one before; each takes longer to heal.

*Cure:* Allow at least one day for each mile of the race as a recovery period. In that time, do no long or hard runs. This, of course, means no racing. Don't race until you've given yourself another day per mile to replace the training lost while you were down for repairs.

*Review:* Chapters 14, 15, and 16 on postrace pains.

**"I took care of all the big things in my training and racing plans. But the little ones fouled me up."**

*Complaint:* You didn't plan for, or adjust your plans for, such things as surface and terrain of the course, the shoes and clothing you wore, food and drink, weather, and travel. One or more unpleasant surprises let you down.

*Cause:* You did not pay attention to detail or were inflexible in the face of sudden change.

*Cure:* Hope for the best, but prepare for the worst. Plan all details, and anticipate all problems.

*Review:* Chapters 7, 8, and 9 on logistics.

## Self-Test 18
## What Did You Forget?

1.  Do you want to race farther, faster, or both? (If you don't answer "yes," you're a rare runner.)

2.  Do you want to train more now? (If you say "no," you can still improve without extra training.)

3.  Did you feel chronically tired in earlier training? (If "yes," keep your rate of progress less than 10 percent a week, alternate hard and easy days, and limit your longest run to about twice your average distance or time.)

4.  Did you feel tired when you started the race? (If "yes," you may not have tapered off enough in training. Cut it in half the last week, and do nothing long or hard.)

5.  Did you lack speed? (If "yes," make sure you speed up to race pace 5 percent of the time in training, and consider racing more regularly.)

6.  Did your starting pace vary dramatically from your finishing pace? (If "yes," try to bring the halves of the race within five seconds per mile of each other by starting faster or slower next time.)

7.  Did the distance seem too far for you, even though you followed the recommended training schedule? (If "yes," make your long runs longer yet, and shorten the short ones or rest on those days.)

8.  Did you run faster in practice than in the race? (If "yes," quit timing yourself in practice. You're wasting your race energy there.)

9.  Did you recover slowly from the race? (If "yes," check to see if you allowed one recovery day per mile of the race before going long or hard again.)

10. Did you get an unwelcome surprise from the course, the weather, your shoes or clothing, etc.? (If "yes," plan logistical details more carefully, and be ready to change plans quickly.)


Note: This test is optional. Take it only if you skipped earlier chapters, ignored their advice, or otherwise failed. Everything here has been asked before.

# Part Three:

# Improving It

# 19

# A Plan for All Seasons

Olympic championships aren't won by the swiftest runners or the strongest, but by the smartest. We have no better recent example than that of a pale and fragile-legged Finn, Lasse Viren. Viren's name isn't on any world-record list, so he isn't the fastest runner. Neither is he the toughest, since he injures himself if he works too hard for too long. Viren wins only at the Olympics—twice in Munich and twice in Montreal. He beats faster, harder-working men by knowing how to do the right training, when to do it, and when to *stop* doing it.

Few reporters give Viren proper credit for what he knows. Few runners—on any level—see that they could go farther and faster, too, if they imitated him.

More than once during the Montreal Olympics, I felt ashamed enough of the way my profession was being practiced that I wanted to burn my press card. Reporters of the Olympics can be forgiven for their excesses of language, for their misplaced emphasis on nationalism, even for their errors of fact. I can excuse their lapses of objectivity and creativity. But I can't let pass their intentionally malicious treatment of Lasse Viren.

Viren regained his winning form about a month before the Games. I was at the Olympic Trials when the news came that he had run a world-leading 10,000. A track writer beside me, who should have known better, nodded and snarled, "He's doped again."

He didn't mean Viren was on heroin or speed. He was implying that the Finn had an extra dose of red blood cells. The rumor was that he had won in 1972 because of "blood doping,"

119

a poorly named technique that involves drawing out and later reinjecting a portion of one's own blood. It's thought to boost the body's oxygen-carrying capacity. When Viren won two races again at Montreal, half-informed journalists immediately swooped down on him like hungry buzzards. They smeared his incredible running with their headlines about "doping."

Viren didn't need medical trickery to win two races in Montreal and to run courageously in the third. If he had a secret, it was not in his blood, but in his training and racing schedules. Viren maintains that he can only stay at a peak for a few weeks, and that when he leaves it he's a long time coming back—four years, if his experiences at Munich and Montreal are any indication.

He says, "Top shape can be planned and timed fairly accurately. And, at least in my case, top shape will stay for a period of about three weeks. It is not possible to conserve good form for a long time in distance running."

After Viren won in the Munich Olympics, he relaxed his training. It must have been embarrassing to him to be beaten easily by people he knew he could have beaten more easily if he'd trained a little more. It must have been worse listening to speculation about how limited he was with his normal blood.

In three years, Viren never came closer than 10 seconds of his best 5,000-meter time or within a half-minute of his 10,000-meter best. But he peaked at the right time, again. Runners who want to win gold medals could learn from him that these races aren't won in the off-years, or even in races two or three months before.

This story wouldn't be too important if its message only applied to Olympians. Like most principles in running, though, it works for everyone; only the specific application changes. The principle here is: if you want to climb the peaks, you must put valleys in between; the higher the peaks, the wider and deeper the valleys.

Viren is the extreme. He spaces his peaks by four years. If you're just trying to improve your times or distances, you may take only a few months between peaks that aren't as high as his because your valleys of recovery aren't as deep. But you still need a Viren-like pattern of highs and lows.

Viren traces his methods to coach Arthur Lydiard, who says, "You can't race well the year-round because your condition will only take you so far. When you're racing hard, you can't train hard. If you compromise, you can hold your form for three or four months. But [then] you're going to have to go back and start to build up again."

This is another way of saying there must be times for building up and times for tearing down. Each has its season. Yet some runners, either by choice or commitment, try to race in all seasons. This appears to be impossible without sacrificing either training background or maximum racing edge.

Overracing is tempting to nearly all distance runners, with the lure of cross-country, indoor and outdoor track, and road races. Races are available all year, and they're hard to resist. But they take a toll. The longer the distance being raced, the more training background a runner needs and the longer it takes to recover afterward. If the schedule leans too heavily on racing, corners are cut in training and in rebuilding.

Few, if any, runners can race at their best in all four seasons. Most, apparently, can't even operate well in two or three consecutive hard seasons, because they can't reap and sow at the same time.

Lydiard says a racer can hold his form for "three or four months" before going back and starting to sow new racing seeds. Tom Osler has reached the same conclusion. Osler writes, in *The Conditioning of Distance Runners,* "One can rarely maintain the high performance level for more than three months or when symptoms of energy depletion are first observed." Osler has found that his running goes in roughly six-month cycles. Each has one high period of about three months and one low period of the same length. He finds the highs best for serious racing, the lows best for basic training and relaxing.

I've noticed I have the same kind of cycles. I used to write it off as coincidence that I came down with an injury or illness every six months or so. But I didn't realize until later that these ailments followed a consistent, predictable pattern: broken down for a few weeks, building back up for a month or so, good running for a couple of months, struggling to hold that peak, and breaking down again. I needed an easy period every few months. If I didn't take it voluntarily, my body ordered it for me.

Osler tells us to identify and cooperate with these up and down periods: "The six-month cycle is of importance to the runner for several reasons. For one, it allows him to predict which times of the year he will perform best. Likewise, it allows him to determine when he should take a less serious attitude toward racing."

My best racing almost always has come in the spring and fall. My ailments and slumps have come in the winter and summer. I suspect that some recycling could have maximized the former tendency and minimized the latter. Every runner can benefit from alternating hard and easy "seasons" the way we now mix hard and easy days.

This part of the book tells how to run and race during a hard season. But don't let the word *hard* scare you. You won't so much train harder as train *smarter*. The work will be more single-minded and concentrated than before, but it shouldn't be too difficult a step up for anyone who has trained with me this far.

So far, I've assumed that you have sampled many kinds of races—here a two-miler on the track, there a 10-miler on the road. Good. This is how you discover which races you perform and like the best. I hope, too, that you raced them on training that didn't change much from event to event, or from season to season. You raced pretty well without special training.

Now, I can tell you how to race much better by specializing for a little while. I can show you how to test speed at shorter distances, to run the same distances faster, or to go farther than before. You do it by pointing for a specific race or series of races at a specific time, and by doing special training for it.

Chapters 20 to 27 deal with peaking for speed, distance, or better combinations of the two. Nothing I say is new in principle; I just refine the way the principles apply.

**Seasons and schedules.** Push yourself for a season of the year, preferably spring or fall when weather conditions and racing opportunities are best. Give yourself a three-month schedule. Harder work is easier to take when you know, first, that its results should be dramatic, and second, that you will reduce training again before long.

**Specifics and simulations.** Concentrate on one type of racing—track, cross-country, short road races, or long road races. Don't bounce around. Repeat the shorter races as often as weekly, or build for a single longer one. Also, rehearse the race pace and conditions regularly in practice so they become more familiar.

**Spurts and stops.** Use a crude form of interval training. Take rest breaks—in short runs to go faster, and in long runs to go farther. For short races, keep the proportion of speed at about 5 percent, but make it faster and more formal (measured, timed, and separate from the gentle 90 percent; racing takes the other 5 percent). For long races, make longer training runs less stressful by walking and stretching for about five minutes every half-hour.

**Splits and strategies.** Pace the race even more carefully than before. Divide the race into four equal parts instead of the two I recommended before. For short races, expect the first and last quarters to be slightly faster than the middle two. For long ones, expect the reverse (faster in the middle).

**Shortcuts and savings.** Lose weight. Choose a fast course. Pick a cool, calm day for racing. Train with a group. Train in the hills. Add certain strength and flexibility exercises. Any of these can improve you with little or no extra work.

## Self-Test 19
## Where Do You Go Next?

1. Would you rather concentrate on improving speed or distance? (Choose only one at a time. See chapters 20 and 24 for introductions to each.)

2. In which set of events do you want to specialize now? (Check only one of the following.)

    a. Track, 1-6 miles (see chapter 21)

b. Cross-country, 1-6 miles in natural settings (see chapter 22)

c. Short road, less than 10 miles (see chapter 23)

d. Longer road, 10-20 miles (see chapter 25)

e. Marathon, 26.22 miles (see chapter 26)

f. Ultramarathon, longer than 26.22 miles (see chapter 27)

3. What three-month season do you plan to spend this way? (See reasons for training in seasons in this chapter.)

4. Are you convinced of the need to train faster for short races and longer for long ones? (If not, read chapter 20 or 24 carefully.)

5. Are you prepared to do a primitive form of interval training, stopping to rest occasionally so you can go either faster or farther? (If "no," study chapter 20 or 24.)

6. Are you willing to race more often for short races or less often for long ones? (See chapter 20 or 24 for advice on racing frequency.)

7. Are you ready to back off for an easy season when this one ends and to allow several months before beginning the next hard one? (If "no," reread this chapter.)

# 20

## Training for More Speed

I was just a high school freshman, living in a town of 300 people and going to a school with no track. What did I or anyone there know about training? We did none that year. All we did was race. When we weren't running in real meets, we raced each other on our eight-laps-per-mile grass field. Without warming up, we did an 880. I probably ran 30 timed half-miles that short season. No reputable training book would advise this, but no one in Coin, Iowa, knew any better. So I improved my time from 2:36 to 2:11 in less than two months. My mile came down from 5:51 to 5:09.

Later, I thought I was smart enough to write training books. But never again could I improve as much, as quickly, as when I knew nothing.

I now know that what I did then was foolish. Please don't copy it exactly. I would have hit a wall soon by doing all racing and no training. But I know, too, that a modified form of this is the best way to get faster in a hurry. Within limits, you race faster simply by racing more often.

While researching my first booklet, *Long Slow Distance*, I asked Bob Deines how much speedwork he did. Deines, then twenty-one years old, had missed the 1968 Olympic marathon team by one place. He said he did no speed training, unless I counted his racing as that.

"Regular racing helps keep me sharp," Bob said. "I think that two or three races are sufficient to recover any lost sharpness without any speed training. It works out to an almost exact formula with me. I'm usually a little sluggish in my first fast race. It may take 4:27 to run a mile. But within a week or two, it's sure to be 4:17. The 10-second [per mile] improvement seems to be pretty standard."

My experience matched his. If I hadn't raced or trained fast at all, I needed four to six weeks to climb to a peak and then could stay there for another four to six weeks.

By my last year of high school, I'd learned to train, but still did little speed work outside of races. I started the season with a 4:44 mile. Six weeks later, I ran a 4:22 that felt easier. Thirteen other races were crammed between these two.

The only time I came close to this form again was summer 1968. By then, I was running gently all the time except when I raced. I ran three-mile races each week for a month at 15:42, 15:25, 15:19, and 15:18. The improvement of eight seconds per mile may not look like much, but the last time came as an afterthought—45 minutes after I'd raced a hard mile. This three-miler again seemed easier than the first. The meets ended before I could go faster.

George Young, the only American distance runner to compete in four Olympics, knows a few things about racing and training. He would approve of racing into top shape. Young has said, "There's no better way to get in speedwork than running a race. You talk of speedwork in terms of [repeat] quarter-miles and all those other things, but you don't get the speedwork there that you gain in a race. You just never really reach the pain barrier, or whatever you call it, in any other way than running the race and hurting that way."

## Simulations

In high school, I raced too often—fifteen times in six weeks of my last season. At that rate, I couldn't have recovered well between races, but I got by with it then by being young and innocent. In 1968, I didn't race enough; the summer program ran out before I reached full speed. Both times I was at the mercy of racing schedules.

To race fastest, you have to find the right balance between enough races and too many. If the schedule isn't right—and by "right" I mean an average of one race every week or two all season at short distances—you have to set it right. Cutting down is easiest; you just skip races if you see you're running too many. But what if you don't have enough? What if the schedule only shows two races, six weeks apart? Is there any way to get sharp for them? I know several ways, two of which I *don't* recommend.

The first is time-trials. You clutch your watch and race alone for the full distance. One of two things happens. You may run as fast as you hoped but can't share your triumph with anyone or more likely, you run as hard as in racing, but not nearly as well with no one there to help. Either way, you waste limited racing energy on runs that mean little. I reject time trials as an alternative to races.

Interval training is better, but not by much. If used in small amounts to give a final racing edge, it would be okay. But stay away from the 10 or 20 times 440 variety that is used both to replace endurance training and to imitate racing. There are better ways to do each.

Build basic endurance from gentle running. It still should be 90 percent of your total even as you build speed. If racing doesn't account for another 5 percent, fake it. Do something that combines the good features of races, time-trials, and intervals, but leaves out the bad.

Like most tricks I write about, this one isn't original. A Finn told me of it. The first time I heard a name put on it, it didn't make any sense. Leevi Seppanen called it the "exchange method." He said it originated in Germany and was widely used by the Finns. Perhaps something was lost in the translation of "exchange" from German to Finnish to English. A better name is "change-of-pace" training or "simulated racing." In simplest terms, this is speed work for people who resist conventional interval training, but who still must work on speed. It is a substitute for racing for those who don't have regular chances to race, but won't do time-trials. This training has more continuity than start-and-stop intervals, yet gives more speed than steady running. It mimics races and trials without being as exhausting.

The Finns use "exchange runs" at their race distance or the greater portion of it. But they vary their effort. Some segments are easy and some are as hard as the race itself. But there is never any stopping, walking, or slow recovery running. The run is continuously timed.

For instance, a four-minute miler might run his first quarter in an easy 75 seconds, do a hard 60 on the second lap, another easy 75 on the third, and finish with a hard 60 for a total time of 4:30. The run can be split all sorts of ways. But the principle is that it combines racing efforts with partial recoveries.

Simulated racing is based on two important and somewhat conflicting facts:

1. Training is specific. To do much good it has to be similar to the race both in terms of distance and pace.
2. It can be too similar. In other words, you can't run an all-out race every day, so maximum efforts must be rationed.

Apparently, training runs of roughly racing distance and an average effort of 90 percent (a pace 30-40 seconds per mile slower than all-out) is specific enough to do some good, yet mild enough not to invite breakdowns. The simulated races accomplish this, and probably do it better than steady-paced efforts because part of the run is at full race tempo.

I've told you about hard-easy days and weeks, and hard-easy seasons. This puts the same principle into a single, short run. Set it up like this:

1. Take a full racing warmup—including at least a half-hour of gentle running, stretching exercises, and striding at race pace—before starting the simulated race.
2. Do it on a surface and terrain that the race itself will have (track, cross-country, or road).
3. Use the shortest distance you'll run this season (for instance, one mile on the track, two miles of cross-country, four miles of short road racing).
4. Estimate the total time that the race would take if you ran it today (examples: 5:00 mile, 11:00 two-mile, 24:00 four-mile).
5. Divide the distance and the time into four equal parts (examples: 440s in 75 seconds for the mile, half-miles in 2:40 for the two-mile, miles in 6:00 for the four-mile).
6. Alternate easy, hard, easy, hard quarters.
7. Run the hard quarters at full racing pace (examples:

second and fourth segments at 75 seconds, 2:45 and 6:00 for one, two, and four miles).

8. Add a total of 30-40 seconds per mile (15-20 seconds per mile each) to the easy quarters (examples: first and fourth parts at 90-95 seconds, 3:15-3:25 and 7:00-7:20 for one, two, and four miles).

9. Cool down as you would after a race.

10. Allow at least *one* day per mile (half the postrace amount) to recover and rebuild before racing or simulating it again.

### Spurts

Are you still with me after that blizzard of numbers? If you followed them, you saw that we're missing some running. I ask you to give 90 percent of your time to gentle running, and 5 percent to races or simulations. The remaining 5 percent is for spurting.

I speed up for one minute in each twenty. I do it every day except when I'm hurting, and I'd keep doing it even if I never raced. I ask you to try it as much as an on-the-move stretching exercise as true speedwork. The legs grow tight from hours of short striding, and this is a simple antidote.

Normally, I glance at my watch, accelerate for a minute to a pace that gets me up off my heels and a little out of breath, and then drop back to gentle running. I just blend this into a long run every so often. It's literally a refreshing change of pace.

However, if I were training to race, I'd be more careful about this. I'd plan the spurts this way:

1. Separate them from the basic run with short rest breaks.

2. Take them when completely warmed up from at least a half-hour of running.

3. Run some of them on the surface and terrain of the race (track, cross-country, or road, depending on the season).

4. Go known distances (220, 330, or 440 yards, for instance) for time sometimes.

5. Do these at the current pace of the shortest race (which probably means faster than before).

## Shortcuts

Two shortcuts are bounce and weight. The first has to do with the connection between jumping ability and speed.

Anyone who knows me knows I'm no Bill Walton. Friends who run with me know, too, that I'm no Valeriy Borzov. In size and speed, I'm about as far from these two as anyone can be. I'm stretching to reach 5½ feet. But 20 years ago, I was a basketball-playing fanatic. Looking back on it now, I see that the way we played built more running strength than basketball skill, since the undisciplined games often went on for 6-8 hours at a time. Despite my shortness, I developed enough jumping power to graze the rim with my fingertips on a good day. I was never a slam-dunker, but I was rather proud of the spring my legs had.

I also thought well of my speed. I once ran a hundred in 10.6 and a quarter in 52.2. While these don't buy much in the sprint market, they are nice for a distance runner to have in reserve. A few years ago, I asked coach Arthur Lydiard about the spring-speed connection and how much each could improve.

"Speed comes from here," the New Zealander said, slapping his upper legs. "Here and the ankles." He demonstrated by springing into the air with a powerful push from his ankles.

He said that to use speed that is inborn and to translate trained-in endurance into speed you must be able to drive strongly with the thigh muscles, lift with the knees, and shoot off of "whippy" ankles. Again, though he was dressed in a business suit, he showed what he meant.

"This is the purpose of our hill training," Lydiard said. He has always advised a few weeks of fast uphill and downhill running as a transition period between endurance training and the racing season. It probably is the most misunderstood and most often ignored part of his schedule. Yet to hear him talk, it's as important as the high-mileage weeks and speed work.

The mistake runners make, he said, is that they try to sprint up the hills. Lydiard said raw speed doesn't count for much here. The emphasis is on strength-building, and this comes from *springing* up hills. The action is as vertical as it is horizontal, giving special attention to the drive of the thighs, the lift of the knees, and the "whip" of the ankles.

If you don't have hills or tend to get hurt on hills, you can even practice this form other ways (like playing basketball). It's just that the hills do the job faster and better. They don't let you cheat.

Arthur Lydiard didn't try to put into numbers the improvement one might expect as the new bounce translates into speed. Tom Osler is more precise when he talks about weight loss. Osler can gain weight just by reading food labels in supermarkets. He has gone up and down in weight so much and so often that he knows its effects to the second and the pound.

"I lose two seconds per mile for each excess pound of body fat," he says.

He isn't alone in this. Until you read otherwise, plan to race 10 seconds faster in a mile if you shed five surplus pounds. The reward grows as you go longer. It's twenty seconds in two miles, fifty in five, 1:40 in 10, and so on.


### Self-Test 20
### How Fast Do You Go?

1.  What set of races do you plan to run this season? (Track, cross-country, or short road?)

2.  What is the shortest of these that you'll race? (In miles; use this as a standard for setting your distance and pace for "simulated races" and timed "spurts.")

3.  What is your current time for this distance? (Estimate if necessary.)

4.  What is the 440-yard pace for this race? (Use this, and equivalent times at other distances, for timed spurts.)

5.  What is one-fourth of your shortest racing distance? (Divide the figure in question 2 by four.)

6.  What is one-fourth of your time for the shortest racing distance? (Divide the figure in question 3 by four.)

7.    What is the "easy factor" for a simulated race? (Multiply the shortest racing distance in miles by 30 to 40 seconds.)

8.    What is the total time for a simulated race? (Add the figure in question 7 to the time in question 3.)

9.    What are your times for the hard segments—second and fourth quarters—of a simulated race? (Use the time in question 6—full race pace.).

10.   What are your times for the easy segments—first and third quarters—of a simulated race? (Divide the easy factor in question 7 equally into the two easy segments.)

# 21

## Racing on the Track

It was fitting that the track meet be on Memorial Day, since so many of my old memories are linked to the track. I've raced there enough times—nearly 400—to recognize the love-hate feelings I have for this kind of running. The track is at once the best and worst place to race. To appreciate the best of it, we first have to recognize the worst.

Juha Vaatainen, a Finn who was the best track runner in the world in 1971, said then, "I don't like to go around a track. Outside of competition, I never do it. Actually, stadiums were invented for spectators, not runners. We have nature, and that's much better."

The standard 440-yard or 400-meter track is artificial—a place no thinking runner would go except to compete, and then only for a few laps. Going around in circles is boring even when you're racing well. When things go poorly, it's painful because there is no place to hide; spectators can watch your every step. You know you must race on a track for your times to count, and you resent the track for making you suffer so much.

On the other hand, track racing has a mathematical perfection and a simplicity that cross-country and road runs lack. You can time every lap; these compare accurately with those from any other track, since one is about like any other. You don't have to worry about knowing the course; just keep making left turns and you can't get lost. When you race well, there's no better place to display yourself since you're never out of sight. Above all, track racing has nostalgic overtones for longtime runners, because most of us started here.

Like Juha Vaatainen, I never train on tracks. I have more natural places to run. But sometimes I race there, if only to refresh old memories. I came back to the track that Memorial Day because I remembered the good too well and had forgotten the bad.

I remembered racing in the state championship mile seventeen years earlier, hearing perfect splits called for the first three laps, sprinting into the lead at just the right place, and coming home in record time to the cheers of the crowd.

I'd forgotten the stark terror that precedes a track race but no other . . . the early jostling for position that throws a little guy like me around like a leaf in a whirlwind . . . the pained breathing that starts almost immediately . . . the rigor mortis that eventually sets in and feels worse than any marathon "wall". . . being recognized and called by name each time I pass the stands, and being asked to give more than I can.

This was a scheduled 10,000-meter race. Mine ended somewhat earlier, the victim of too fast a start, 80-degree heat, blisters, and calf cramps. But it didn't end before I caught glimpses of my old self out there on the track. The promise of such sights will bring me back again.

## Schedule

Here are some notes on training and racing for the track season:

- Make it a full three months. The spring of the year usually offers the most track meets; summer is next.
- Give a slightly different emphasis to each of the months. The first month (weeks 1-4) is a "break-in" month in which you claim or reclaim speed without making too abrupt a shift; start with simulated races instead of the real thing. The second month (weeks 5-9) is a "build-up" month in which racing begins and the pace increases quickly. The third month (weeks 10-13) is a "hold-on" month; racing pace level levels off, but you can maintain this high level for awhile.
- Don't start this program until you have averaged 30 or more minutes of running a day for a couple of months.

- Alternate easy and hard days, as recommended earlier (chapter 4). There are three of each per week, with one day left "optional" for rest or for making up missed training. Keep doing 90 percent of your running at a gentle pace. This season it maintains your endurance, and is a warmup for, and cool-down from, faster running.

- Replace the longest weekly run with an actual or simulated race. Simulate at the distance of the shortest race. (See chapter 20 for details.) Make the speed work more formal on the other two hard days by separating it from the basic distance run, running it on the track for time and recovering well between spurts. On easy days, simply blend the spurts into the long runs. Train at the current pace of your shortest race in all speed work; this should improve as the season progresses.

- Combine just three different sessions: easy—30-minute runs, including 3 x 30 seconds fast; harder—60-minute runs, plus 3 x 440 on the track for time; hardest—a race or simulation, plus up to 60 minutes of gentle running for warmup and cool-down (see sample).

### Table 4
### Track Season Training

| Day | Suggested Training |
| --- | --- |
| 1 | 30 minutes (including 3 x 30 seconds fast) |
| 2 | 30 minutes; 3 x 440 yards fast (timed on track); 30 minutes* |
| 3 | 30 minutes (including 3 x 30 seconds fast) |
| 4 | 30 minutes; 3 x 440 yards fast (timed on track); 30 minutes* |
| 5 | 30 minutes (including 3 x 30 seconds fast) |
| 6 | up to 30 minutes; race or simulation; up to 30 minutes |
| 7 | optional (rest or makeup day) |

*If the previous week's race was three miles or longer, replace one or both of these sessions with an easy 30-minute run.

Note: This applies to the entire three months of the track season.

- Race only on the track this season. While you can cover the full 1- to 6-mile range, the training here is designed more specifically for races taking less than a half-hour to complete (usually one, two, and three miles or their metric equivalents). Concentrate on these distances. Specialize in *one* event (for instance, the mile) in the second month, then race other distances after your time in the main one plateaus out.
- Taper (lighten the week's training significantly) only before the one or two biggest races of the season. Otherwise, you'd always be tapering.
- If races are three miles or longer, give yourself more recovery time than provided here. Take only the "easy" sessions until one day has passed for each mile of racing, and don't race again until you've put in two days per mile.

## Splits

Here are some notes on pacing races on the track.

- Track pacing is both easier and harder than pacing races elsewhere. It is easier because you hear your times every lap, with every lap the same distance as every other. Pacing on the track is harder because each second in these short races means much more than it does in longer ones. You must pace yourself precisely on the track.
- The principles given in chapter 11 still apply, with further refinements. It's still important that you run the first half like a "scientist" and the last half like an "artist." Keep the time of the two halves as close to each other as possible. Now, however, cut each half into two pieces. Plan to run the first and last quarters of the race a little faster than the middle two. This recognizes that you move out quicker than even pace in track races, slow in the middle half, and then speed up again as you sniff the finish. Accept a modest faster-slower-faster pattern as normal.
- I've done some of the figuring for you. The pacing tables in this chapter have a built-in 1 percent difference between faster and slower laps. Now, simply find how fast you expect to race, and check how fast your early, middle, and late laps should be.

## Table 5
## Track Race Pacing

| Mile Pace | Average Lap Times (seconds) | 1st & 4th Quarter Lap Times (seconds) | 2nd & 3rd Quarter Lap Times (seconds) |
|---|---|---|---|
| 4:00 | 60.0 | 58.8 | 61.2 |
| 4:10 | 62.5 | 61.2 | 63.8 |
| 4:20 | 65.0 | 63.7 | 66.3 |
| 4:30 | 67.5 | 66.1 | 68.9 |
| 4:40 | 70.0 | 68.6 | 71.4 |
| 4:50 | 72.5 | 71.0 | 74.0 |
| 5:00 | 75.0 | 73.5 | 76.5 |
| 5:10 | 77.5 | 75.9 | 79.1 |
| 5:20 | 80.0 | 78.4 | 81.6 |
| 5:30 | 82.5 | 80.8 | 84.2 |
| 5:40 | 85.0 | 83.3 | 86.7 |
| 5:50 | 87.5 | 85.7 | 89.3 |
| 6:00 | 90.0 | 88.2 | 91.8 |
| 6:10 | 92.5 | 90.6 | 94.4 |
| 6:20 | 95.0 | 93.1 | 96.9 |
| 6:30 | 97.5 | 95.5 | 99.5 |
| 6:40 | 100.0 | 98.0 | 102.0 |
| 6:50 | 102.5 | 100.4 | 104.6 |
| 7:00 | 105.0 | 102.9 | 107.1 |
| 7:10 | 107.5 | 105.3 | 109.7 |
| 7:20 | 110.0 | 107.8 | 112.2 |
| 7:30 | 112.5 | 110.2 | 114.8 |
| 7:40 | 115.0 | 112.7 | 117.3 |
| 7:50 | 117.5 | 115.1 | 119.9 |

Note: First, find the *average* pace you plan to run in columns one and two. Then, multiply the *adjusted* paces in columns two and three by the number of laps in each one-fourth of the race (or the nearest distance where times are given). Add the first-quarter time to the second to get a projected half-way time, and add the third-quarter time to that. The accompanying chart for the mile shows cumulative "splits" computed this way, with times converted to minutes and seconds.

- The difference in pace between faster and slower quarters should only be about 1 percent. The first and last segments take 24.5 percent of the total time, while the middle segments take 25.5 percent. This doesn't sound like much difference, but it amounts to a significant 3 seconds per lap in a five-minute mile and 14 seconds per mile in a 36-minute six-mile.

## Table 6
### Pacing the Mile

| Time for the Mile | One-Lap Time | Two-Lap Time | Three-Lap Time |
|---|---|---|---|
| 4:00 | 59 sec. | 2:00 | 3:01 |
| 4:10 | 1:02 | 2:05 | 3:08 |
| 4:20 | 1:04 | 2:10 | 3:16 |
| 4:30 | 1:06 | 2:15 | 3:24 |
| 4:40 | 1:09 | 2:20 | 3:31 |
| 4:50 | 1:11 | 2:25 | 3:39 |
| 5:00 | 1:13 | 2:30 | 3:47 |
| 5:10 | 1:16 | 2:35 | 3:54 |
| 5:20 | 1:18 | 2:40 | 4:02 |
| 5:30 | 1:21 | 2:45 | 4:09 |
| 5:40 | 1:23 | 2:50 | 4:17 |
| 5:50 | 1:26 | 2:55 | 4:24 |
| 6:00 | 1:28 | 3:00 | 4:32 |
| 6:10 | 1:31 | 3:05 | 4:39 |
| 6:20 | 1:33 | 3:10 | 4:47 |
| 6:30 | 1:36 | 3:15 | 4:54 |
| 6:40 | 1:38 | 3:20 | 5:02 |
| 6:50 | 1:40 | 3:25 | 5:10 |
| 7:00 | 1:43 | 3:30 | 5:17 |
| 7:10 | 1:45 | 3:35 | 5:25 |
| 7:20 | 1:48 | 3:40 | 5:32 |
| 7:30 | 1:50 | 3:45 | 5:40 |
| 7:40 | 1:53 | 3:50 | 5:47 |
| 7:50 | 1:55 | 3:55 | 5:55 |

• You don't need to be as exact as I imply. Times within a couple of seconds of those listed are close enough. Also, it isn't practical to get times at exact one-fourth distances—for instance, after each 1.85 laps of a 3,000-meter run. This isn't necessary. Just note the closest full-lap times: laps 1-2-3 of a mile or 1,500 meters; laps 2-4-6 of two miles or 3,000 meters; laps 3-6-9 of three miles or 5,000 meters; and laps 6-12-18 of six miles or 10,000 meters.

### Self-Test 21
### How Do You Train and Race?

Write a three-month (thirteen-week) schedule for the track season, basing it on the sample week in this chapter. Also, answer the following as the season goes on:

1. What was your average pace for the timed 440s each week? (Run them at your current pace for the shortest race.)

| Week | Time | Week | Time | Week | Time |
|---|---|---|---|---|---|
| 1 | ____ | 6 | ____ | 11 | ____ |
| 2 | ____ | 7 | ____ | 12 | ____ |
| 3 | ____ | 8 | ____ | 13 | ____ |
| 4 | ____ | 9 | ____ | | |
| 5 | ____ | 10 | ____ | | |

2. What were your "simulated race" paces for the hard and easy segments? (I recommend one a week for the first four weeks—at your shortest racing distance. The second and fourth parts should be at full racing pace, with the first and third parts 30 to 40 seconds per mile slower.)

| Week | Distance | 2 Hard Parts | 2 Easy Parts |
|---|---|---|---|
| 1 | ____ | ____ | ____ |
| 2 | ____ | ____ | ____ |
| 3 | ____ | ____ | ____ |
| 4 | ____ | ____ | ____ |

3.  What races did you run? (I recommend one a week for week 5 to 13.)

| Week | Distance | Time | Week | Distance | Time |
|------|----------|------|------|----------|------|
| 5 | ____ | ____ | 10 | ____ | ____ |
| 6 | ____ | ____ | 11 | ____ | ____ |
| 7 | ____ | ____ | 12 | ____ | ____ |
| 8 | ____ | ____ | 13 | ____ | ____ |
| 9 | ____ | ____ | | | |

4.  What was your average pace per lap for each quarter of the race? (The steadier your pace the better, though you can expect the first and fourth quarters to be slightly faster than the middle two.)

| Week | Distance | First | Second | Third | Fourth |
|------|----------|-------|--------|-------|--------|
| 5 | ____ | ____ | ____ | ____ | ____ |
| 6 | ____ | ____ | ____ | ____ | ____ |
| 7 | ____ | ____ | ____ | ____ | ____ |
| 8 | ____ | ____ | ____ | ____ | ____ |
| 9 | ____ | ____ | ____ | ____ | ____ |
| 10 | ____ | ____ | ____ | ____ | ____ |
| 11 | ____ | ____ | ____ | ____ | ____ |
| 12 | ____ | ____ | ____ | ____ | ____ |
| 13 | ____ | ____ | ____ | ____ | ____ |

5.  What personal records did you set?

| Week | Distance | New/Old Times |
|------|----------|---------------|
| ____ | ____ | ____ |
| ____ | ____ | ____ |
| ____ | ____ | ____ |
| ____ | ____ | ____ |
| ____ | ____ | ____ |
| ____ | ____ | ____ |

# 22

# Racing over the Country

Hardly anyone takes cross-country as seriously as the other aspects of the sport. Unlike track and road racing, this kind seems to lead nowhere. It offers nothing comparable to the Olympic Games or the Boston Marathon. The season is short and has few races worthy of hard, concentrated training. No one is a cross-country specialist. No one keeps comparative lists of cross-country times, since courses vary so much in distance and difficulty. No one besides the runners themselves pays this season much attention.

And maybe that's the point of it. This season is meant to be an interlude, something different from the roads and tracks, a break from concerns with splits and PRs, and a chance to get away from crowds and to get our feet back on real earth.

Track people must spend most of the year running in circles on ovals designed for spectators and coated with rubber for speed. Road runners escape the confining track, but use even harder surfaces on courses designed for, and shared by, cars. Distances are standard enough so anyone, anywhere, anytime can compare results. Road and track racers become very time-conscious.

Cross-country provides an excuse to escape from all of this for a while. To be true cross-country, it must be run on natural surfaces—dirt, grass, or sand. If it's natural, it almost surely is not smooth and flat. The rougher it is, the harder the work of measuring it and running it—and the less the times mean. The more natural the course is, the more we are at the mercy of the weather. Cross-country is as unpredictable as the season between summer and winter. It may start in 100-degree heat that has burned the grass brown and sucked the ground so dry that runners in front of you kick up choking dust. The season may end, not two months later, as you plow through four inches of snow with your spit freezing on your chin.

In between the extremes, though, you may be treated to the most glorious running days of the year—chilly but sunny October mornings when your feet crash through brittle leaves before biting into firm, damp soil. These rare days that I've never found outside of the cross-country season are enough to make a poet of anyone.

The courses are no more standard than the weather. If you hear a track race will be three miles long, you know practically everything about it. The distance tells you almost nothing about cross-country. First, that distance could be anything from 2.8 to 3.3 miles. The course could go through a city park in New York, around a golf course in Kentucky, across a cornfield in Iowa, along a Rocky Mountain trail in Colorado, through a desert in New Mexico, or on a beach in California. It could have one hill lasting the whole distance, or the biggest rise might be a footbridge on the eighteenth fairway.

Cross-country is never standard. It's as varied as the places it is run, and it can be run almost anywhere. The one common element is that all the terrain is natural. For a change, we must face surfaces and terrains on their terms instead of using those modified for our ease and speed. Cross-country at its best is not a race with the clock, but with the elements.

## Schedule

Here are some notes on training and racing during the cross-country season:

- It should last three full months (13 weeks). This almost surely will be autumn in the United States, since most races are at that time of year. The first month the emphasis is on breaking in solely with simulated races. Racing begins the second month, and the pace builds up quickly. It levels off and you hold on in the the third month.

## Table 7
## Cross-Country Season Training

| Day | Suggested Training |
|-----|--------------------|
| 1 | 30 minutes (including 3 x 30 seconds fast) |
| 2 | 30 minutes, 3 x 440 yards (timed on a measured portion of cross-country course); 30 minutes* |
| 3 | 30 minutes (including 3 x 30 seconds fast) |
| 4 | 30 minutes; 3 x 440 yards (timed on a measured portion of cross-country course); 30 minutes* |
| 5 | 30 minutes (including 3 x 30 seconds fast) |
| 6 | up to 30 minutes; *race or simulation;* up to 30 minutes |
| 7 | optional (rest or makeup day) |

*If the previous week's race was three miles or longer, replace one or both of these sessions with an easy 30-minute run.

Note: This schedule applies to the full three months of cross-country season.

- Most features of the schedule are like they were for track (chapter 21): pretraining at least 30 minutes a day for several months; alternating hard and easy days all season; 90 percent of the running at a gentle pace; replacing the longest run of the week with a race or simulation; making "spurts" more formal (measured and timed) on two days each week and blended into gentle runs the other days; doing all speed training at the pace of the shortest race.

- The schedule (see sample) uses just three sessions: easy—30-minute runs including 3 x 30 seconds fast; harder—60-minute runs plus 3 x 440 on a cross-country course for time; hardest— a race or simulation, plus up to 60 minutes of gentle running for warmup or cool-down.

- The only real difference between cross-country and track training is *place*. The distances are about the same, so the schedules look alike in amount and style. But the change of place makes them much different in substance. With hills and soft, uneven ground, cross-country training is as different from track work as a mountain hike is from a city stroll.

- You get ready for hills and rough going just as you adapt to faster track speeds—by making them more familiar. Start by making them an everyday part of your training menu. Do more (or all) of your normal, gentle running on "natural" surfaces and terrains. Here, you partially adjust to cross-country's demands without really trying.

- You try much harder, of course, in specialized speed training. For your twice-a-week timed spurts, lay out a representative section of course—preferably with some up- and downhill running. Make it about a quarter-mile. The exact distance isn't important; all you need is one place for taking and comparing times all season.

- Simulate your race for the first four weeks of the season, and on non-racing weeks after that. Run these rehearsals on a racelike course and at the shortest racing distance. Divide the course into four approximately equal parts. Do the second and fourth at full race pace, and the first and third at a total of 30-40 seconds per mile slower. (You'll probably have to estimate both distance and pace. Run what feels right.)

- All racing this season should be on cross-country courses. Keep the distances in the 2- to 6-mile range—the shorter the better so you can race more often. Ideally, the races should take less than 30 minutes. Race weekly if events are three miles or less, and every other week if they are longer than that. Reduce the recommended training only the week before the one or two most important races of the season.

### Strategies

Here are some notes on cross-country racing tactics:

- Nowhere else in running is it more important to "read" a course before you race it. I strongly recommend running the whole thing in advance so you'll know all of its tricks. Race a course more than once if possible. Each experience teaches you ways to save time your next race.

- Track and cross-country distances are about the same, but the racing requirements aren't. Endurance, strength, and—above all—hill running technique are more vital in the country than raw speed.

- Generally, take this attitude about hills: keep the *effort* constant, but let the pace shift with the grade. For instance, you might be running a six-minute effort up a steep hill, but shift down to an eight-minute pace. Going down the other side, you shift up to five-minute pace, but maintain the six-minute effort.

- Specifically, run hills this way: lean into the hill with your whole body as you climb, springing from the ankles and toes, and driving powerfully with the arms. Glide down hills, letting gravity do some of the work as you try to keep your body perpendicular to the ground.

- The changes in surface and terrain dictate a more flexible pace than you'd run on the track or roads. Plan on doing more surging and slowing than you would elsewhere. For this and other reasons (notably inaccurate measurements), split times mean little in cross-country. Either ignore what you hear, or don't let it influence you too much. Run what *feels* right for the conditions instead of what appears right from the watch. This, of course, is a main purpose of cross-country; to get you away from counting every second.

### Self-Test 22
### How Did You Train and Race?

Write a three-month (13-week) schedule for the cross-country season, basing it on the sample week in this chapter. Also, answer the following as the season goes on:

1.  What was your average pace for timed "spurts" in training? (I recommend using a single course of about 440 yards all season.)

Distance

| Week | Time | Week | Time | Week | Time |
|------|------|------|------|------|------|
| 1 | ____ | 6 | ____ | 10 | ____ |
| 2 | ____ | 7 | ____ | 11 | ____ |
| 3 | ____ | 8 | ____ | 12 | ____ |
| 4 | ____ | 9 | ____ | 13 | ____ |
| 5 | ____ | 10 | ____ | | |

2.  What were your "simulated race" times and paces? (Run one a week for the first month and possibly others later. Times should be 30-40 seconds per mile slower than current race pace but with some segments as fast as races.)

| Week | Distance | Pace per Mile |
|------|----------|---------------|
| 1 | ____ | ____ |
| 2 | ____ | ____ |
| 3 | ____ | ____ |
| 4 | ____ | ____ |

3.  What races did you run? (Try to run at least one every other week during the second and third months of the season.)

| Week | Distance | Time | Pace per Mile |
|------|----------|------|---------------|
| 5 | ____ | ____ | ____ |
| 6 | ____ | ____ | ____ |
| 7 | ____ | ____ | ____ |
| 8 | ____ | ____ | ____ |
| 9 | ____ | ____ | ____ |
| 10 | ____ | ____ | ____ |
| 11 | ____ | ____ | ____ |
| 12 | ____ | ____ | ____ |
| 13 | ____ | ____ | ____ |

# 23

# Racing the Short Roads

It reminded me of the way races used to be but rarely get to be anymore. It was just the right distance at 10 kilometers and just the right size at no more than 100 runners. It never felt too fast or too long, and I never felt crowded or alone. I think this is about as far as races should be most of the time. This is only about one-fourth of a marathon. Most runners would gain as much from racing 10 kilometers as plodding a marathon—probably more because they could run the short ones four times as often.

I also think this is as big as most races should get. They are better in almost every sense when only a hundred or so people run them. I'm not saying everyone else should go away. I'm saying we should have more races and not more runners per race. Instead of putting 10,000 people in one event, divide that many into 100 different events. Then, everyone could have more running room, the director could handle the crowd, the traffic could still get through, and we could all enjoy the race and each other a lot more.

Unfortunately, the twin manias for distance and size now work against this kind of racing. They give the impression that races aren't worthy of consideration unless they approach marathon length or draw four-figure fields. Races of less than 10 miles, those taking less than an hour to run, don't interest a true long-distance runner very much. They get in the way of his training by causing his mileage to drop on race days. So he rarely races these distances.

Only oddities bring crowds to short races: the chance to be

part of a mob scene; the chance to climb the face of a mountain; the chance to race at all in mid-winter or mid-summer
when it is too risky to go farther.

There isn't much demand now for the kind of race I ran in
Hollister, California: an uncrowded 10 kilometers on a nearly
flat, fast course, run in perfect weather. There aren't many
chances to run for time at a distance where going fast means
more than going far. I can't name more than half a dozen
opportunities a year like this in an area that supports that many
races each weekend. The ones that are this short are either too
big, too steep, or too lax in organization.

Yet I can't think of a better place for a mildly serious runner
to spend his time. This is the ideal range for someone who
wants to race often and pretty well, and still not suffer too
much for it. These distances don't require the hard speed training of track, the hours on the roads of marathoning, or the
grinding hill work of cross-country. The races don't usually
result in the paralysis of oxygen debt that you feel on the
track, and you don't hit the "wall" of the marathon or the
hilly, swampy ground of the country. Unlike the longer races,
you can run these every couple of weeks. Unlike the shorter
ones, you don't have to do too much extra speed work between
races to stay sharp enough.

All of the elements are here—some speed, some distance,
some hills—without the extremes of any. I've been to the
extremes of all three kinds of racing. Small, simple 5- to 10-
milers are the places I've decided to settle down. If I want to
make rare trips out from here again, I'm familiar enough with
the other neighborhoods to visit them briefly. But this is home.

## Schedule

Here are some notes on training and racing during the short
road-race season:

- Race only on the roads and only in this distance range this
  season. The races can be anything less than 10 miles but, in
  fact, usually should take at least 30 minutes and not longer
  than an hour to run.

- These are middle-distance or "transition" races—not short
  anymore, but not yet very long. The training and racing

plans borrow features from both the shorter and longer distances, but are unique in their combinations of speed and endurance running.

## Table 8
## Short Road Season Training

Training Weeks

| Day | Suggested Training |
|-----|--------------------|
| 1 | 30 minutes (including 3 x 30 seconds fast) |
| 2 | 30 minutes; half-mile (timed on a measured portion of road course); 30 minutes |
| 3 | 30 minutes (including 3 x 30 seconds fast) |
| 4 | 30 minutes; half-mile (timed on a measured portion of road course); 30 minutes |
| 5 | 30 minutes (including 3 x 30 seconds fast) |
| 6 | 1 hour 30 minutes (fast spurts are optional) |
| 7 | optional (rest or makeup day) |

Racing Weeks

| Day | Suggested Training |
|-----|--------------------|
| 1 | 30 minutes (including 3 x 30 seconds fast) |
| 2 | 30 minutes; half-mile (timed on a measured portion of road course); 30 minutes |
| 3 | 30 minutes (including 3 x 30 seconds fast) |
| 4 | 30 minutes (including 3 x 30 seconds fast) |
| 5 | 30 minutes (including 3 x 30 seconds fast) |
| 6 | up to 30 minutes; race; up to 30 minutes |
| 7 | optional (rest or makeup day) |

Recovery Weeks

Run easy 30 to 45 minutes daily until one day for each mile of the race has passed; then begin a "training week."

Note: This schedule applies to the full three months of the short road-racing season. The recommended cycle is three weeks—one for training, one for racing, and one for recovery.

- The schedule remains like track and cross-country in these ways: (a) a three-month, 13-week season; (b) alternating easy and hard, short and long days, with one day a week left optional for rest or makeup; (c) one day of recovery running for each mile of the race; (d) "spurts" done at the pace of the shortest race; and (e) 90 percent of the running at a gentle pace.

- Modifications of the plans from shorter, faster races are: (a) somewhat more running—40-45 minutes a day instead of the 35-40 recommended earlier; average in the thirties before starting this program; (b) instead of race simulations, substitute timed half-miles twice a week on a measured road course that you use all season; (c) run fewer races, since you go farther and recovery takes longer.

- The new features for this season are: (a) three-week cycles—a training week, a racing week, and a recovery week; (b) long runs of twice the daily average in training weeks to build extra endurance for the longer races; (c) a slight tapering of training to freshen up for races.

- The schedule (see sample) combines four types of runs: easy-short—30 minutes including 3 x 30 seconds fast; hard-long—60 minutes plus a half-mile on the road for time; longest—90 minutes; hardest—race plus up to 60 minutes of warmup and cool-down.

## Splits

Here are some notes on pacing the short road-races:

- These occupy a middle ground between track and cross-country. Splits come less often and mean less than they do in track, but are more frequent, accurate, and valuable than in cross-country. Road courses generally are marked at some or all mile points—even when the full distance is metric. The first mile and the one nearest to halfway are most important so you can first settle into an appropriate pace and later judge how evenly you paced the halves.

- Don't count on hearing your times yelled at these points, or even finding anyone there to yell them. If you depend on splits, wear a watch and check your own time.

151

## Table 9
## Pacing 10 Kilometers

| Running Time | One-Mile Time | Three-Mile Time |
|---|---|---|
| 30 minutes | 4:49 | 14:29 |
| 31 minutes | 4:59 | 14:58 |
| 32 minutes | 5:09 | 15:27 |
| 33 minutes | 5:18 | 15:55 |
| 34 minutes | 5:28 | 16:24 |
| 35 minutes | 5:37 | 16:53 |
| 36 minutes | 5:47 | 17:22 |
| 37 minutes | 5:57 | 17:51 |
| 38 minutes | 6:07 | 18:21 |
| 39 minutes | 6:17 | 18:50 |
| 40 minutes | 6:26 | 19:19 |
| 41 minutes | 6:36 | 19:48 |
| 42 minutes | 6:46 | 20:17 |
| 43 minutes | 6:55 | 20:46 |
| 44 minutes | 7:05 | 21:14 |
| 45 minutes | 7:14 | 21:43 |
| 46 minutes | 7:24 | 22:12 |
| 47 minutes | 7:34 | 22:41 |
| 48 minutes | 7:43 | 23:10 |
| 49 minutes | 7:53 | 23:39 |
| 50 minutes | 8:03 | 24:09 |
| 51 minutes | 8:12 | 24:37 |
| 52 minutes | 8:22 | 25:06 |
| 53 minutes | 8:31 | 25:35 |
| 54 minutes | 8:41 | 26:04 |
| 55 minutes | 8:51 | 26:33 |
| 56 minutes | 9:00 | 27:01 |
| 57 minutes | 9:10 | 27:30 |
| 58 minutes | 9:19 | 27:59 |
| 59 minutes | 9:29 | 28:28 |

Note: This commonly run event is a strange hybrid. Though the full distance is metric, the splits usually are given at mile distances. The chart solves some of the confusion. The splits indicate exact even-paced running. Of course, they can vary by several seconds per mile in the race, and your final time won't suffer.

● These should be the most evenly paced races. They don't have the fast-start-and-finish pattern of speed races, or the late slowdown brought on by extreme distance. Each mile should be paced very much alike. The half-times, of course, would then be within a few seconds per mile of equal.

### Self-Test 23
### How Did You Train and Race?

Write a three-month (13-week) schedule for the short road-racing season, basing it on the sample weeks in this chapter. Also, answer the following as the season goes on:

1.  What was your average pace for the timed half-miles each week? (I recommend using a single road course for these all season to give an accurate comparison of times.)

| Week | Time | Week | Time | Week | Time |
|------|------|------|------|------|------|
| 1 | ___ | 6 | ___ | 11 | ___ |
| 2 | ___ | 7 | ___ | 12 | ___ |
| 3 | ___ | 8 | ___ | 13 | ___ |
| 4 | ___ | 9 | ___ | | |
| 5 | ___ | 10 | ___ | | |

2.  What races did you run? (Try to do one about every third week, or four or five during the season.)

| Week | Distance | Time | Pace per Mile |
|------|----------|------|---------------|
| ___ | ___ | ___ | ___ |
| ___ | ___ | ___ | ___ |

3.  What were your pacing patterns? (Subtract the fast-half time from the slow-half time, and divide the difference by the race distance. The resulting figure should be less than five seconds per mile.)

| Week | Distance | First Half | Second Half | Sec. per Mile |
|------|----------|-----------|-------------|---------------|
| ___ | ___ | ___ | ___ | ___ |
| ___ | ___ | ___ | ___ | ___ |

4.  What personal records did you set?

| Week | Distance | New/Old Times |
|------|----------|---------------|
| ___ | ___ | ___ |

# 24

## Training for More Distance

A young writer came to me for advice as I worked on this book. He asked, "How do you discipline yourself to write a book? I can do articles okay, but a book seems to be so much work for such a long time that it frightens me away from starting."

I told him, "I don't write books. I write separate two-page articles—two pages today, two new ones tomorrow, and so on. I can't look much beyond tomorrow's work or I'd be scared, too. But if I keep writing these small pieces, they eventually add up to a book."

The easiest way to do any kind of drawn-out work, in writing or running, is to break it into smaller pieces. This is the principle behind interval training. By alternating work with recovery, you go farther, faster, or both than you could in one straight shot.

Anyone who thinks of me as Mr. LSD may be shocked to hear this, but I believe in and use interval training all the time. Not only that, I think it offers even more to a runner who wants to go longer than to one who's trying to go faster. The intervals I'm talking about are small building blocks laid together run after run until they form a solid foundation. No single block is that tough by itself, but the final structure can stand up to enormous beatings.

Running a 10- to 20-mile race, a marathon, or an ultramarathon means taking such a beating. Yet it's wrong to think you must prepare for it by beating out those distances all the time. If you put together the right kind and number of intervals, you never need to train as far as you race.

Of the thousands of people who finish marathons, for instance, very few ever have gone that far outside of their races. They know they get in shape easier by running small portions of the races over and over again—building from the bottom—than by stretching occasionally to the top of their distance range.

The peak distance goes up automatically as the average distance of the pieces increases. This has to do with something rather unpleasantly named the "collapse-point theory." Ken Young, an American record-holder in several ultramarathon distances, devised the formula. He says that the point at which one breaks down in a long-distance race will be about one-twentieth of his total mileage for the past two months. In other words, if you logged 400 miles during that period and you're trying to race a marathon, you may be in trouble after twenty miles. (Twenty miles is one-twentieth of four hundred.) Young uses two months' training as a basis, because that's about how long it takes to accumulate the desired training effects from all the miles.

There's a simpler way of expressing Young's formula, while still avoiding tampering with its basic premise: reduce the mileage to a daily average. Tripling that average gives the same collapse point as Young's original method.

The practical significance is this: if you want to finish a race before the physical resources run dry, plan on averaging at least one-third of its distance per day for eight weeks before the race. Beyond the collapse point lurks not only drastic slowdowns and dropouts, but potential injuries from severely depleted reserves.

A common weekly average for marathoners is 50 miles a week. That's 7 miles each day. Triple that, and the collapse point is about 21 miles. Young doesn't think it is coincidental that "so many low-mileage runners hit the wall around 20 miles of a marathon."

He says:

> I would emphasize that these are basically absolute minimums. You can't expect to go farther than the collapse distance even under the *best* conditions (of weather and terrain). And under typical conditions, you may collapse before this point. Also, if the collapse point is close to the racing distance, the runner is only going to be

able to cover the distance without collapsing. This does not mean
he is going to be able to race well at six miles, for example, by
maintaining two miles a day. He will just be able to cover six miles.

Young admits that the theory first came from his own
racing experience. But after his articles appeared in *Runner's
World,* he picked up statistical backing.

Paul Slovic, of the Oregon Research Institute, found in a
detailed study of several hundred marathoners that those who
had more substantial training background held up better toward
the end and therefore had faster times. The entire field averaged
42 miles a week, or 6 a day, in the eight weeks before the race,
according to Slovic. But the men finishing under three hours
were doing about 9 miles a day, compared to 5 miles for the
slower runners. The sub-three group had a projected collapse
point of 27 miles; the over-threes could expect trouble after
15 miles.

Slovic matched pace for the first 10 miles against the last
six-plus. All runners slowed somewhat. But in the sub-three-
hour group the slowdown averaged 14 percent, while in the
lighter trainers it was almost three times as great—40 percent!
Slovic then separated the runners breaking 2:45. They trained
10 miles a day, putting their collapse point farther beyond
marathon distance. The average drop in pace for these runners
was only 8½ percent.

If Ken Young hadn't already spelled out the collapse-point
theory (which now has a wide following), we could dismiss him
as a crank when he attacks one of the sacred cows of long-
distance running. Young does not place much stock in the long
weekend run—the 20-plus-miler on the roads, which has been
traditional since the early 1960s. It isn't a prerequisite to racing
success; it isn't even a very efficient way to train, according to
Ken. He should know. He bashed out many thirty- and forty-
milers before realizing there was a better way to extend his
"collapse" distance.

"It took me two years to increase my collapse point from 20
to 30 miles using this method," he says. "But after realizing the
correlation between total mileage and collapse, I added roughly
20 miles to my collapse point in 1½ years."

He did so by upping his average. He tested the idea on himself and wrote before the Boston Marathon:

> My longest run in the last two months (since an early February marathon) has been a 15-mile race. Previous to that, I had no runs longer than 16 miles since Dec. 1 [the day he ran his fastest marathon of 2:29]. Thus, I go into Boston with only two runs—both races—of 20-plus miles in eight months. However, in that time I have averaged 106 miles per week.
>
> My theory is that repeat hard runs of 10-15 miles—say, four such over a weekend—are superior to the same total distance in fewer, longer runs. On one recent weekend, I ran my 12.3-mile course four times. Of course, Boston will provide the test of the theory, so we'll see.

Young wrote me another long letter after Boston. "I think I have substantiated (at least to my satisfaction) the essential tenet of the collapse-point theory," he said. "It is *average* mileage which is important in determining the collapse distance. It is virtually immaterial whether one runs two 12-milers in one day or one 24-miler—at least in determining the collapse point. This means a runner can concentrate on his speed (e.g., two faster 12-milers) rather than waste effort in longer, slower, perhaps harder runs."

The reason Ken was so sure of his position was that he'd taken no runs longer than fifteen miles in the two months before Boston, and yet he improved his best marathon time by 3½ minutes—to 2:25:41. His collapse point was 45 miles.

"My weekend training partner, Eric Groon, had been training similarly, but without any runs longer than 15 miles for the preceding four months, no marathons within two years. His calculated collapse point was 32 miles. He ran 2:30:16, his best by 17 minutes."

Young added:

> I doubt that most runners will accept this theory, and hence won't make use of it. The idea that long runs are necessary is too ingrained in their thinking. I used to do long runs (30-plus miles) monthly or so, but it took a lot of mental preparation/stamina. I think these runs actually made me *less* prepared mentally for long races.
>
> Doing my weekend running in 12½-mile bites, they are easier to face, easier to recover from, and I run them much faster than I would otherwise. How else could I get in a fairly concentrated two-day 50 miles at six-minute pace?
>
> I feel that the super-distance fad is a compensation for lack of

understanding of basic training principles. "Just pile on mileage and you too can be a super runner," the thinking goes. Many runners cannot handle the mileage without breaking down physically.

I doubt that I'll ever run more than 20 miles in a workout again. I'll save my mental stamina for races, where it counts.

## Schedules

Forget the big numbers—like four 12-mile runs in a weekend at six-minute pace—that Ken Young uses. Few of us have his ability or would run that far even if we could. Just remember his "collapse-point" principle. Even by doing the minimum amount, most of us can go farther, faster than ever before.

My purposes, then, in this and the next three chapters are: (1) to see how far you can go on modest training, not to find out how much work you can tolerate; (2) to extend the distance you can hold at a good pace, not to increase your speed as such. You get faster at these distances not by building speed but by gaining the strength to keep going. You get that by taking many intervals of one-third the racing distance.

**Collapse Points.** Everything revolves around the longest race of the season and the daily running average. Divide the racing distance by three. That's what you must average each day in training if you plan to race as fast or faster than you train. (If you go slower, you might get by on a one-fourth average. But I'm assuming you want to push the pace.)

These are the minimum training distances for different races:

| Your Longest Race | Daily Average |
| --- | --- |
| 20 kilometers/half-marathon | 4½ miles |
| 15 miles/25 kilometers | 5¼ miles |
| 30 kilometers/20 miles | 6¾ miles |
| Marathon | 8¾ miles |

While I list these in miles for the sake of convenience, keep running by periods of time if you normally do it that way. Simply average one-third of the *time* you expect to take in the race.

The daily averages are based on seven-day weeks, even if you don't run every day. Divide each week's total distance or time by seven for your average. Some runs will, of course, be shorter or longer than that. Maintain the minimum of one-third the racing amount for six to eight weeks before racing. This gives you time to adapt fully to the new load.

**Long Runs.** I agree with Ken Young that we don't need extra-long training runs. But I think reasonably long ones are still important for several reasons:

- They boost the average. Running twice as much as usual on one day means we can do less on one, or more on others.
- They build confidence. If we never ran beyond a third of the race in practice, we'd wonder where the other two-thirds would come from.
- They burn fat. The best way I know to keep my weight down without dieting is to run for two hours.
- They make the other runs easier. After going two hours on a weekend, a weekday hour seems to pass in no time.

Run for twice the daily average—or two-thirds of the season's longest race distance. It's long enough to help in all these ways but not so long that it hurts badly. The distances to train for each race are as follows:

| Your Longest Race | Longest Run |
|---|---|
| 20 kilometers/half-marathon | 9 miles |
| 15 miles/25 kilometers | 10½ miles |
| 30 kilometers/20 miles | 13½ miles |
| Marathon | 17½ miles |

**Progress.** You can safely double your amount of running in just six weeks by upping it an average of 10 percent a week (a little faster than that at the start, slower as you near the top).

Start from a base of a half-hour a day. If you aren't already there, go back to chapter 4 and do the prerequisite work. Then climb according to this table:

| Week | Average | Longest |
|---|---|---|
| 1 | 35 minutes | 1:10 |
| 2 | 40 minutes | 1:20 |
| 3 | 45 minutes | 1:30 |
| 4 | 50 minutes | 1:40 |

| Week | Average | Longest |
|------|---------|---------|
| 5 | 55 minutes | 1:50 |
| 6 | 60 minutes | 2:00 |

The total for week six is enough for anyone but marathoners—and many of them do well on this. Shorter-distance racers may want to stop earlier.

**Pace.** Training for distance is as straightforward as can be. You just run the scheduled amounts comfortably. This training pace isn't much different from race pace (though, naturally, the race will be less comfortable at three times the distance)—so you simulate racing every time you run.

You need no special speed work. But I advise keeping "spurts" in your program. Speed up for one minute in each twenty minutes to give your legs a refreshing stretch.

## Shortcut

As often happens, I found this shortcut while looking for something else. I learned how to run longer and easier while trying to relieve an injury.

My left Achilles tendon hurt almost constantly early in 1977. It wasn't a bad pain, and I ran on it as usual while it nagged at me like a dull headache. When I have a pain like this, I usually slow down a little more, cut out racing, and keep going about the same distances as always. In other words, I baby myself only in terms of pace.

Yet about the only pain-free runs I had in six months were the rare short races—half-mile and mile fun-runs. That was the confusing thing. Why should the slowest runs keep hurting and the fastest ones feel best?

This had happened again and again through the years, but only lately had I recognized the pattern. The answer, like many of those that are too long in coming, was simple: I stopped.

The pain went away when I stopped. It was there when I warmed up for races, as it always was on daily runs. But I only warmed up for 15 to 30 minutes. Then I stopped and waited up to 10 minutes more for the race to start. I did some fast, short striding during that time, but I mostly did stretching exercises or just stood around.

When I started to run again, the soreness was usually gone. I'd broken the pain cycle. If I hadn't stopped, it might have kept spiraling upward—or at least stayed constant—as it had on unbroken runs.

A solution to chronic soreness, I finally realized, might be to break up my runs with rest periods in more or less this same way. I already accepted this in principle. My "van Aaken breaks"—named for the man who first convinced me we could gain instead of lose by stopping in mid-run—consisted of pausing at stoplights, to climb fences or to tie my racing shoes. I almost never stopped without such a reason, and I rarely stopped for more than a few seconds. This wasn't long enough. If I hurt before the break, I still hurt after it, because I wasn't stopped long enough for my body to realize it wasn't still running.

I began stopping longer on daily runs almost by accident. The circumstances came together perfectly in June 1977 to teach me an important and dramatic lesson.

I hadn't done my stretching that morning, and I felt stiff and tight. It was early in the run, and the Achilles was hurting more than usual. I was alone, so I wouldn't be breaking up anyone else's routine. I was on a pleasant, isolated stretch of levee where no one could see me if I stopped. And I was in even less of a hurry than usual. Fifteen painful minutes into the run, I stopped, walked a bit, emptied my bladder, did some standing-and-bending stretches, tightened my shoelaces, and walked a little more. The whole break took about five minutes, and the second half of the run was pain-free—which made the time-out an excellent investment.

My only concern with taking breaks like this was what it would do to my timing—in two senses of the word.

I wondered how a rest would affect my rhythm in the few minutes after I started running again. But I needn't have worried. I was smooth as could be—much smoother, in fact, than at any time before the break. I ran an out-and-back course, coming back three minutes faster than I went out—and the faster part was the easier of the two.

Another of my compulsions is keeping track of my running time. I worried that the stops would mess up my records, since I couldn't very well count the time spent walking, standing, and stretching into my totals. That problem was easily solved. I simply made time stand still while I stopped. I checked the time when I took the break, then set the watch back to that number when I began running again. The watch didn't know I'd taken a time-out, but my legs did.

Ken Young says he may never run longer than twenty miles again in training. I may never go beyond thirty minutes without taking a five-minute walk-and-stretch break. I started doing this to ease away pains, but I've kept it up for more positive reasons. This is the best way I know to recover lost training quickly. I once trained back this way from nothing (in a cast for a sprained ankle) to a marathon in two months.

And this is the only way I know to cheat the collapse-point tables. By running intervals, I've gone 70 miles in 14 hours on training that should have stopped me before 30 miles.

Any block of work looks more appealing when we cut it into smaller pieces.

## Self-Test 24
### How Far Do You Go?

1. How far do you plan to race this season? (If 10-20 miles, see chapter 25 for details; if marathon, see chapter 26. These questions don't apply to ultramarathons for reasons given in chapter 27.)

2. What is the minimum amount of training needed for this race? (Divide the distance or your estimated time by three.)

3. How far do you need to go in your longest runs? (Multiply the answer in question 2 by two, which equals two-thirds of the race distance or time.)

4. How much training have you averaged each day for the last eight weeks? (Divide the total amount of miles or minutes by all the days, even if you didn't run everyday.)

5. What is your present "collapse point"? (Multiply the daily average by three.)

6. What have your single longest runs each week averaged in the last eight weeks? (Add them up and divide the total by eight.)

7. How should your daily averages and longest runs progress from where you are now to the amounts you need? (Add about 10 percent a week to each total. See the chart in the "progress" section of this chapter.)

| Week | Average | Longest |
|------|---------|---------|
| 1____ | _____ | _____ |
| 2____ | _____ | _____ |
| 3____ | _____ | _____ |
| 4____ | _____ | _____ |
| 5____ | _____ | _____ |
| 6____ | _____ | _____ |

8. What pace per mile do you expect to hold in the race? (You'll probably train at about this rate but at shorter distances.)

# 25

# Racing Ten to Twenty Miles

I'm here to praise the 25-kilometer run. I know it will never stand beside the marathon or even the 10-K as one of the glamor events. But the sport needs another important race at a distance in between them; the 25-K is almost precisely halfway between.

The difference between 10 kilometers and the marathon—the two longest Olympic races—is too much. They lie 20 miles apart. That's two to three hours of running and two to three times the training requirements. Yet the first thing most runners do after they satisfy themselves that they can race at all is to think, "Now, I want to be a marathoner!" I suppose it's natural, given the urge to go where the most action is.

Frank Shorter crossed the yawning gap in distance and style between the 10,000 and marathon in one great leap. Beginning racers also do it all the time. I would have done it, too, but in 1963 the schedules didn't yet offer a smorgasbord of marathons.

You couldn't drive an hour some weekend to run one. You had to travel to Chicago or one of the coasts. The remoteness of the marathon added to its mystique, and I badly wanted to run one from the moment I subscribed to *Long-Distance Log*. It brought news each month of faraway races that I could only run in my imagination. I was lucky that way. Imagined marathons never hurt like real ones would have for a boy who rarely ran more than thirty miles a week and never had gone longer than two hours.

I went to California that summer looking for races. There

were no marathons, fortunately, but one road race looked like a fair substitute. It was 30 kilometers—the National AAU Championship, in fact. I didn't know exactly how far this was, and only later figured out it was triple my longest race to date but still only three-fourths of a marathon.

We runners, of course, knew nothing about "collapse points" then. We thought all we had to do to run farther was run slower. If we crept along slowly enough, we could run all day.

Compared to my mile racing speed, I seemed to go in slow motion. I wrote later in my diary, "I passed guys most of the way. I was barely moving, but they were barely moving *slower.*"

Then, something happened that I'd never felt before. I knew what it was like to be desperately tired. This wasn't it. From the waist up, everything was fine. My head was clear, my will intact. My damn legs just didn't want to run any more. They became like two redwood logs in the space of a few hundred yards at about the 25-kilometer point. I dragged them in.

My first road race would have been perfect if it had stopped at 25 kilometers. That would have been long enough to show how marathoning felt, but not so long that I would never want to feel it again. Even with a weak finish, I sharpened my appetite for more. This is one reason I say 25 kilometers—give or take a half-hour of running time—is a humane place to begin a marathon experiment. Another reason is that the training needed for it is a convenient compromise between what I recommend for track and for the marathon.

I tell every marathoner-to-be to spend a few months running in this distance range. And I know you're almost sure to ignore me. Okay, so you're as impatient to get on to the "big one" as I was. Promise me this, then: you'll come back later to fill in the gap you left between one and two hours of racing.

## Schedule

Here are some notes on training and racing during the 10 to 20 mile season:

- This season, like all others, lasts three full months or thirteen weeks. Ten and twenty miles are the outside limits of racing. However, I suggest running only those distances that take between one and two hours to finish. The schedule lists three

## Table 10
## Training for the Season

**WEEK ONE**

| Day | Suggested | Actual |
|---|---|---|
| 1 | 30 minutes | ____ |
| 2 | 40 minutes | ____ |
| 3 | 30 minutes | ____ |
| 4 | 45 minutes | ____ |
| 5 | 30 minutes | ____ |
| 6 | 1 hr. 10 min. | ____ |
| 7 | optional | ____ |
| Total | 245 minutes | ____ |
| Average | 35 minutes | ____ |

**WEEK TWO**

| Day | Suggested | Actual |
|---|---|---|
| 1 | 30 minutes | ____ |
| 2 | 55 minutes | ____ |
| 3 | 30 minutes | ____ |
| 4 | 55 minutes | ____ |
| 5 | 30 minutes | ____ |
| 6 | 1 hr. 20 min. | ____ |
| 7 | optional | ____ |
| Total | 280 minutes | ____ |
| Average | 40 minutes | ____ |

**WEEK THREE**

| Day | Suggested | Actual |
|---|---|---|
| 1 | 35 minutes | ____ |
| 2 | 1 hour | ____ |
| 3 | 35 minutes | ____ |
| 4 | 1 hour | ____ |
| 5 | 35 minutes | ____ |
| 6 | 1 hr. 30 min. | ____ |
| 7 | optional | ____ |
| Total | 315 minutes | ____ |
| Average | 45 minutes | ____ |

**WEEK FOUR**

| Day | Suggested | Actual |
|---|---|---|
| 1 | 30 minutes | ____ |
| 2 | 1 hour | ____ |
| 3 | 30 minutes | ____ |
| 4 | 30 minutes | ____ |
| 5 | 30 minutes | ____ |
| 6 | Race 1 to 1½ hrs. | ____ |
| 7 | optional | ____ |
| Total | 250 minutes | ____ |
| Average | 35 minutes | ____ |

**WEEK FIVE**

| Day | Suggested | Actual |
|---|---|---|
| 1 | 30 minutes | ____ |
| 2 | 30 minutes | ____ |
| 3 | 30 minutes | ____ |
| 4 | 40 minutes | ____ |
| 5 | 30 minutes | ____ |
| 6 | 50 minutes | ____ |
| 7 | optional | ____ |
| Total | 210 minutes | ____ |
| Average | 30 minutes | ____ |

**WEEK SIX**

| Day | Suggested | Actual |
|---|---|---|
| 1 | 30 minutes | ____ |
| 2 | 50 minutes | ____ |
| 3 | 30 minutes | ____ |
| 4 | 50 minutes | ____ |
| 5 | 30 minutes | ____ |
| 6 | 1 hr. 30 min. | ____ |
| 7 | optional | ____ |
| Total | 280 minutes | ____ |
| Average | 40 minutes | ____ |

166

## WEEK SEVEN

| Day | Suggested | Actual |
|---|---|---|
| 1 | 35 minutes | _____ |
| 2 | 1 hour | _____ |
| 3 | 35 minutes | _____ |
| 4 | 1 hour | _____ |
| 5 | 35 minutes | _____ |
| 6 | 1 hr. 30 min. | _____ |
| 7 | optional | _____ |
| Total | 315 minutes | _____ |
| Average | 45 minutes | _____ |

## WEEK EIGHT

| Day | Suggested | Actual |
|---|---|---|
| 1 | 30 minutes | _____ |
| 2 | 1 hour | _____ |
| 3 | 30 minutes | _____ |
| 4 | 30 minutes | _____ |
| 5 | 30 minutes | _____ |
| 6 | Race 1½ hr. | _____ |
| 7 | optional | _____ |
| Total | 280 minutes | _____ |
| Average | 40 minutes | _____ |

## WEEK NINE

| Day | Suggested | Actual |
|---|---|---|
| 1 | 30 minutes | _____ |
| 2 | 30 minutes | _____ |
| 3 | 30 minutes | _____ |
| 4 | 40 minutes | _____ |
| 5 | 30 minutes | _____ |
| 6 | 50 minutes | _____ |
| 7 | optional | _____ |
| Total | 210 minutes | _____ |
| Average | 30 minutes | _____ |

## WEEK TEN

| Day | Suggested | Actual |
|---|---|---|
| 1 | 30 minutes | _____ |
| 2 | 50 minutes | _____ |
| 3 | 30 minutes | _____ |
| 4 | 50 minutes | _____ |
| 5 | 30 minutes | _____ |
| 6 | 1 hr. 30 min. | _____ |
| 7 | optional | _____ |
| Total | 280 minutes | _____ |
| Average | 40 minutes | _____ |

## WEEK ELEVEN

| Day | Suggested | Actual |
|---|---|---|
| 1 | 35 minutes | _____ |
| 2 | 1 hour | _____ |
| 3 | 35 minutes | _____ |
| 4 | 1 hour | _____ |
| 5 | 35 minutes | _____ |
| 6 | 1 hr. 30 min. | _____ |
| 7 | optional | _____ |
| Total | 315 minutes | _____ |
| Average | 45 minutes | _____ |

## WEEK TWELVE

| Day | Suggested | Actual |
|---|---|---|
| 1 | 35 minutes | _____ |
| 2 | 1 hour | _____ |
| 3 | 35 minutes | _____ |
| 4 | 1 hour | _____ |
| 5 | 35 minutes | _____ |
| 6 | 1 hr. 30 min. | _____ |
| 7 | optional | _____ |
| Total | 315 minutes | _____ |
| Average | 45 minutes | _____ |

## WEEK THIRTEEN

| Day | Suggested | Actual |
|---|---|---|
| 1 | 30 minutes | _____ |
| 2 | 60 minutes | _____ |
| 3 | 30 minutes | _____ |
| 4 | 30 minutes | _____ |
| 5 | 30 minutes | _____ |
| 6 | Race 1½ to 2 hrs. | _____ |
| 7 | optional | _____ |
| Total | 280 minutes | _____ |
| Average | 40 minutes | _____ |

races at monthly intervals, each longer than the last. The first is 1 to 1½ hours, the second about 1½ hours, and the third in the 1½ to 2 hour range.

• Enter the program only if you are averaging at least 30 minutes a day. If you're doing less, use the schedule in chapter 4 to reach this minimum. If you're already doing 40 or more minutes a day, skip buildup weeks one and two.

• By week 13, you will have averaged about 40 minutes a day for the season. This gives a "collapse point" of 40 x 3 = 120 minutes, or enough to carry you through races lasting as long as two hours.

• The runs alternate between long and short—three of each with one "optional" day of week for rest or for making up missed training. Short runs are about one-tenth of the week's total, long runs two-tenths, and longest runs three-tenths.

• Train at a pace you feel you could maintain for your longest race. Spurts—increases in pace for about one minute in every twenty—aren't required, but are recommended. Spurts help keep the legs alive and loose during long runs, and for this reason, are more valuable than speed work.

• Respect the increased stresses of longer races. Taper down your training for several days before racing. Then allow the usual one easy day per mile after the race for recovery and another day to rebuild. The schedule provides all of this.

## Splits

Here are notes on pacing and tactics for the 1 to 2 hour races:

• In these events, completing the distance is the main concern; doing it fast is secondary. In shorter races, smart pacing makes the difference between a faster or slower finish. At this distance, pacing makes the difference between finishing and dropping out.

• Because the early miles seem easy, the great temptation is to push the pace. But don't! Hold back and treat the first quarter of the race as little more than a warmup. Allow the pace to lag a few seconds per mile behind the average time you hope to run. You can make up that much and more in the middle miles, where you do your real racing. Put some time in reserve there for the last quarter, where you hang on with whatever strength and will you have left. The pace may slow again near the end.

- The pacing tables reverse the pattern of the speed races. Here, the middle portions are about 1 percent *faster* than those at the start and finish. Splits usually are read at five-mile intervals, so adjust your time schedules to those checkpoints.

### Table 11
### Long Race Pacing

| Average Per Mile | 1st- & 4th- Quarter Pace | 2nd- & 3rd- Quarter Pace |
|---|---|---|
| 5:00 | 5:06 | 4:54 |
| 5:15 | 5:21 | 5:09 |
| 5:30 | 5:37 | 5:23 |
| 5:45 | 5:52 | 5:38 |
| 6:00 | 6:07 | 5:53 |
| 6:15 | 6:23 | 6:07 |
| 6:30 | 6:38 | 6:22 |
| 6:45 | 6:53 | 6:37 |
| 7:00 | 7:08 | 6:52 |
| 7:15 | 7:24 | 7:06 |
| 7:30 | 7:39 | 7:21 |
| 7:45 | 7:54 | 7:36 |
| 8:00 | 8:10 | 7:50 |
| 8:15 | 8:25 | 8:05 |
| 8:30 | 8:40 | 8:20 |
| 8:45 | 8:56 | 8:34 |
| 9:00 | 9:11 | 8:49 |
| 9:15 | 9:26 | 9:04 |
| 9:30 | 9:41 | 9:19 |
| 9:45 | 9:57 | 9:33 |

Note: Using the race's time checkpoints, divide the distance in nearly four equal parts. Figure your overall pace from column one, the pace for the starting and ending segments from column two, and the middle quarters from column three. The accompanying chart does this for the frequently run half-marathon in which only five- and ten-mile times are read.

## Table 12
## Pacing Half a Marathon

| Time for Race | 5-Mile Time | 10-Mile Time |
|---|---|---|
| 1:10 | 26:55 | 53:25 |
| 1:15 | 28:55 | 27:15 |
| 1:20 | 30:50 | 1:01:00 |
| 1:25 | 32:45 | 1:04:50 |
| 1:30 | 34:40 | 1:08:40 |
| 1:35 | 36:35 | 1:12:30 |
| 1:40 | 38:30 | 1:16:20 |
| 1:45 | 40:25 | 1:20:05 |
| 1:50 | 42:20 | 1:23:55 |
| 1:55 | 44:15 | 1:27:45 |
| 2:00 | 46:10 | 1:31:35 |
| 2:05 | 48:10 | 1:35:20 |
| 2:10 | 50:05 | 1:39:10 |

## Self-Test 25
## How Did You Train and Race?

Fill in the training schedule given for this season, or write an adjusted one for yourself. Also, answer the following questions as the season goes along.

1. What were your "collapse points" (CPs) week by week? (Multiply your average daily amount of running over the past eight weeks by three. Your next race time shouldn't exceed this total.)

| Week | CP | Week | CP | Week | CP |
|---|---|---|---|---|---|
| 1 | ___ | 6 | ___ | 11 | ___ |
| 2 | ___ | 7 | ___ | 12 | ___ |
| 3 | ___ | 8 | ___ | 13 | ___ |
| 4 | ___ | 9 | ___ | | |
| 5 | ___ | 10 | ___ | | |

2. How long was your longest run each week? (It should be at least two-thirds as long as the next race you plan to run.)

| Week | Longest | Week | Longest | Week | Longest |
|------|---------|------|---------|------|---------|
| 1 | ___ | 6 | ___ | 11 | ___ |
| 2 | ___ | 7 | ___ | 12 | ___ |
| 3 | ___ | 8 | ___ | 13 | ___ |
| 4 | ___ | 9 | ___ | | |
| 5 | ___ | 10 | ___ | | |

3. What were your race results?

| Week | Distance | Time | Pace per Mile |
|------|----------|------|---------------|
| ___ | ___ | ___ | ___ |
| ___ | ___ | ___ | ___ |
| ___ | ___ | ___ | ___ |

4. How well did you pace these races? (Estimate the times for each half. Subtract the fast half from the slow half. Divide the difference by the race distance in miles. The result should be less than five seconds per mile.)

| Race | 1st Half | 2nd Half | Sec. per Mile |
|------|----------|----------|---------------|
| ___ | ___ | ___ | ___ |
| ___ | ___ | ___ | ___ |
| ___ | ___ | ___ | ___ |
| ___ | ___ | ___ | ___ |
| ___ | ___ | ___ | ___ |

# 26

# Racing the Marathon

BOSTON, MONDAY, APRIL 17, 1978–"Good morning," the operator droned in the mechanical way that hotel wake-up callers talk. "It is 6:30. The temperature outside is 44 degrees."

I looked out at the same dark grayness that Boston had all of this weekend. I thought of all the happy runners in town this morning and was glad for them—and a little jealous that they drew a good day, while I'd picked two of the sunniest and hottest to run in '76 and '77.

I thought, too, of how the Boston Marathon had changed for me—how eleven years ago I'd used most of my savings to fly cross-country to Boston; how I'd dreamed of doing it again for the next eight Aprils but couldn't afford to, and how most of the country's marathoners still pay to go or wish they could.

Now, I'm paid to go there *not* to run. I was asked to go and write a story about what I saw, and of course I said yes. I wanted to be there, and yet I was a little uneasy about this new role. I would walk the edges of the marathon instead of running in it. I would pose as an expert among thousands of true experts—those who have earned their way here by their training and racing. Would I see the Boston Marathon without feeling it?

**7 a.m.** He meant well, this marathoner on his way to breakfast. He waved me down as I ran up Boylston Street and said, "I don't mean to give advice, but there's a much better place . . ." He motioned toward the Charles River and its bordering bike path, Boston's running thoroughfare.

I said, "Thanks, I've been there. But I prefer the streets today." I couldn't have run anywhere else on marathon day but the last few miles of the course. This was my weak symbolic link with all those who have gone this way before and would do it again this afternoon.

**8 a.m.** "Rodgers, Shorter, and a Cast of Thousands" read the headline in the paper. To read the papers, or hear radio and television, you'd think this was all the Boston Marathon meant—a few stars followed by a faceless mob. But I didn't look at it that way. The quality and size held some interest, but the true appeal of this event was the chance to look into the crowd and pick out individual faces I recognized, and shout encouragement to them before they moved away. It would be my small way of paying back the people who'd picked me out of the crowd in races past and told me I did something more than help fill the road behind the stars.

**11 a.m.** Hawkers and gawkers competed with runners for space near the new starting line behind Doughboy Statue on Route 135. Helicopters buzzed overhead like flies above a picnic, and a hot-air balloon on the ground advertised a light beer. Runners warmed up without needing to, just to keep from exploding with excitement. They talked without saying anything just to make the time go faster. They looked for friends they'd promised to meet but would never find in this crowd. It looked aimless and chaotic, but was simply a larger version of the choreographed routine runners go through before all races.

**Noon.** The radio announcer called the start through my transistor as I hurried toward the car several blocks away, into a cold wind that would later push the runners. I didn't mind missing the start any more than I'd miss seeing the finish. Replays of both would go on all night and half of the next day. The first and last yards are only warmups and victory laps, anyway. The part of the marathon I wanted to see was the most real part to me—the middle and late miles as they are run by the people in the middle and at the back of the pack.

**12:45 p.m.** The front-runners raced through the nine-mile point in Natick before we reporters could drive there. Thirty or forty of them had passed before we found a viewing spot beside Route 135. I stood and watched, awed, as most of the parade passed by. I looked at the faces in the crowd. All of those beautiful faces—so healthy, so positive, so eager. I connected names with many of them and called them out. First, the runners jerked their heads around toward a familiar sound in a strange place. Then they smiled to think, "Hey, somebody knows I'm here!"

**2:10 p.m.** Man beat machine. Our car was stopped on the wrong side of the Prudential Center when the word came:

"It's Rodgers. Bill Rodgers is running the last 100 yards to the finish line as he wins his second Boston Marathon. But another runner is close. He's 50, no 35 . . . only about 25 yards back. But Rodgers holds him off. Jeff Wells is second."

This race was over, and I hadn't seen any of it. But the marathon was a long way from done.

**2:25 p.m.** After a mile of broken-field running, notebook and pen in one hand, radio in the other, I found a small opening in the crowd along Commonwealth Avenue and claimed it. I guessed 150 runners had passed this point at about 25½ miles. Thousand were yet to come.

**4 p.m.** The sub-four-hour runners were done, and I must have seen at least 4,000 of them. I called to those I knew, but I didn't expect any response at this point. The faces had changed in the last two to three hours of running. As they came by individually instead of in the earlier clumps, I saw the frozen stares runners have in the last mile of a marathon. It's the mixture of effort laid down already and anticipation of what lies around just two more turns.

I saw myself pass by hundreds of times, and it made me very proud I was a runner, too. I don't say anyone was made in my image. I only say we're unique parts of a big family with similar roots. We'd read the same stories, felt the same joys and pains, run the same paths, and this was the result. We all came away better for having been here together.

I may have helped make someone's day by yelling from the sidewalk. But these people made mine 4,000 times greater by running past so fast.

I left my spot beside the road and walked past the finish line toward my hotel. All along, I saw runners wincing as they tried to move legs that had worked so well just a little while earlier. I heard pieces of conversations:

"I finally got under . . ."

"My best by eight minutes . . ."

"I can't believe it . . ."

"PR . . ."

"PR . . ."

"PR . . ."

Only someone close to running could understand how they could be so sore and so happy all at once.

**5 p.m.** The evening *Globe* with its story on the race arrived at the hotel and sold out within minutes. All of the local television stations and the three networks covered the race. ABC's story dealt with the fad, the fashions, and the business of running. The sport had those elements, but they weren't the point today.

**The next morning.** The only thing moving fast in Boston that morning was the newspapers. The *Globe* did its usual thorough job in reporting the race—from its three-page list of all the entrants on Sunday to its four pages of stories and results today—so the papers went quickly. They were the best souvenirs in town.

I went out at 6 a.m. to make sure I'd have my copy, and even then I had to run two miles for it. Few runners were out, and those I saw weren't doing a very good imitation of a run. Their limps were their badges of courage.

I needed the *Globe* to tell me what I hadn't seen and heard while I was busy being more of a spectator than a reporter. I assumed my view was complete and accurate until I saw the editorial page. An anonymous observer, who must have been angry about being stranded in marathon traffic on Monday, wrote:

"Long-distance running is the new sublimation, the ultimate in deferred gratification. It is a monkish pastime, best suited to those who would live their lives after a fixed routine of daily hours on the road and lonely nights wolfing down great gobs of carbohydrates to build up reserves of glycogen, then falling sound asleep. For his own protection, the marathoner must develop an infinite capacity to endure boredom."

The writer either didn't see or seriously misread the faces I saw there. The ones I saw didn't display boredom, but first great purpose, and then great delight. These people didn't run in monkish isolation, but shared strength with each other and those of us who only watched.

## Schedule

Twice in 1978 I watched big marathons. After Boston, I saw the Mayor Daley race in Chicago. Together, these races had more than 10,000 runners, and I felt like a teacher on graduation day as they passed. I didn't know one runner in a hundred, and no more than that noticed the little guy beside the road with a goofy smile frozen on his face. But that didn't stop me from being proud of them. Some of these runners were my students, whether we knew it or not.

I had written a marathon training schedule and published it so many places that it was rather widely used. I'd started some of these people training for their first marathons. Now I had a chance to see them finish. That made me proud—not of myself, but of them. Anyone can write a schedule, but it takes a special person to make it work to create a new marathoner where none had been before. I'm flattered that so many special people have chosen to use my program. It first appeared in the February 1977 *Runner's World,* and since then, with slight modifications, in two books and two magazines. I print it again here.

The plan has two premises. First, in as little as three months of training, you too can finish a marathon. Second, you can do it by averaging only an hour of training a day. I'm not saying you'll run the distance fast. But on the other hand, I'm not saying you have to suffer as much as faster runners do, either in training or the race.

I haven't written a note anywhere saying, "Let me know how your marathon goes." Yet I hear from ten people a month who followed the program. Of those who have written so far, more ran over four hours than under three. (The range is 2:49 to 5:06, with most times clumped around 3:40.) However, the figure that delights me most is that only one runner in more than one hundred said he had to drop out of his marathon.

## Table 13
### Marathon Season Training

WEEK ONE

| Day | Suggested | Actual |
|---|---|---|
| 1 | 25 minutes | _____ |
| 2 | 50 minutes | _____ |
| 3 | 25 minutes | _____ |
| 4 | 50 minutes | _____ |
| 5 | 25 minutes | _____ |
| 6 | 1 hr. 10 min. | _____ |
| 7 | optional | _____ |
| Total | 245 minutes | _____ |
| Average | 35 minutes | _____ |

WEEK TWO

| Day | Suggested | Actual |
|---|---|---|
| 1 | 30 minutes | _____ |
| 2 | 55 minutes | _____ |
| 3 | 30 minutes | _____ |
| 4 | 55 minutes | _____ |
| 5 | 30 minutes | _____ |
| 6 | 1 hr. 20 min. | _____ |
| 7 | optional | _____ |
| Total | 280 minutes | _____ |
| Average | 40 minutes | _____ |

WEEK THREE

| Day | Suggested | Actual |
|---|---|---|
| 1 | 35 minutes | _____ |
| 2 | 1 hour | _____ |
| 3 | 35 minutes | _____ |
| 4 | 1 hour | _____ |
| 5 | 35 minutes | _____ |
| 6 | 1 hr. 30 min. | _____ |
| 7 | optional | _____ |
| Total | 315 minutes | _____ |
| Average | 45 minutes | _____ |

WEEK FOUR

| Day | Suggested | Actual |
|---|---|---|
| 1 | 35 minutes | _____ |
| 2 | 1 hr. 10 min. | _____ |
| 3 | 35 minutes | _____ |
| 4 | 1 hr. 10 min. | _____ |
| 5 | 35 minutes | _____ |
| 6 | 1 hr. 45 min. | _____ |
| 7 | optional | _____ |
| Total | 350 minutes | _____ |
| Average | 50 minutes | _____ |

WEEK FIVE

| Day | Suggested | Actual |
|---|---|---|
| 1 | 40 minutes | _____ |
| 2 | 1 hr. 20 min. | _____ |
| 3 | 40 minutes | _____ |
| 4 | 1 hr. 20 min. | _____ |
| 5 | 40 minutes | _____ |
| 6 | 1 hr. 45 min. | _____ |
| 7 | optional | _____ |
| Total | 385 minutes | _____ |
| Average | 55 minutes | _____ |

WEEK SIX

| Day | Suggested | Actual |
|---|---|---|
| 1 | 40 minutes | _____ |
| 2 | 1 hr. 30 min. | _____ |
| 3 | 40 minutes | _____ |
| 4 | 1 hr. 30 min. | _____ |
| 5 | 40 minutes | _____ |
| 6 | 2 hours | _____ |
| 7 | optional | _____ |
| Total | 420 minutes | _____ |
| Average | 1 hour | _____ |

## WEEK SEVEN

| Day | Suggested | Actual |
|---|---|---|
| 1 | 40 minutes | _____ |
| 2 | 1 hr. 30 min. | _____ |
| 3 | 40 minutes | _____ |
| 4 | 1 hr. 30 min. | _____ |
| 5 | 40 minutes | _____ |
| 6 | 2 hours | _____ |
| 7 | optional | _____ |
| Total | 420 minutes | _____ |
| Average | 1 hour | _____ |

## WEEK EIGHT

| Day | Suggested | Actual |
|---|---|---|
| 1 | 40 minutes | _____ |
| 2 | 1 hr. 30 min. | _____ |
| 3 | 40 minutes | _____ |
| 4 | 1 hr. 30 min. | _____ |
| 5 | 40 minutes | _____ |
| 6 | 2 hours | _____ |
| 7 | optional | _____ |
| Total | 420 minutes | _____ |
| Average | 1 hour | _____ |

## WEEK NINE

| Day | Suggested | Actual |
|---|---|---|
| 1 | 40 minutes | _____ |
| 2 | 1 hr. 30 min. | _____ |
| 3 | 40 minutes | _____ |
| 4 | 1 hr. 30 min. | _____ |
| 5 | 40 minutes | _____ |
| 6 | 2 hours | _____ |
| 7 | optional | _____ |
| Total | 420 minutes | _____ |
| Average | 1 hour | _____ |

## WEEK TEN

| Day | Suggested | Actual |
|---|---|---|
| 1 | 40 minutes | _____ |
| 2 | 1 hr. 30 min. | _____ |
| 3 | 40 minutes | _____ |
| 4 | 1 hr. 30 min. | _____ |
| 5 | 40 minutes | _____ |
| 6 | 2 hours | _____ |
| 7 | optional | _____ |
| Total | 420 minutes | _____ |
| Average | 1 hour | _____ |

## WEEK ELEVEN

| Day | Suggested | Actual |
|---|---|---|
| 1 | 40 minutes | _____ |
| 2 | 1 hr. 30 min. | _____ |
| 3 | 40 minutes | _____ |
| 4 | 1 hr. 30 min. | _____ |
| 5 | 40 minutes | _____ |
| 6 | 2 hrs. 30 min. | _____ |
| 7 | optional | _____ |
| Total | 450 minutes | _____ |
| Average | 1 hr. 5 min. | _____ |

## WEEK TWELVE

| Day | Suggested | Actual |
|---|---|---|
| 1 | 40 minutes | _____ |
| 2 | 1 hr. 30 min. | _____ |
| 3 | 40 minutes | _____ |
| 4 | 1 hr. 30 min. | _____ |
| 5 | 40 minutes | _____ |
| 6 | 2 hours | _____ |
| 7 | optional | _____ |
| Total | 420 minutes | _____ |
| Average | 1 hour | _____ |

## WEEK THIRTEEN

| Day | Suggested | Actual |
|---|---|---|
| 1 | 30 minutes | _____ |
| 2 | 30 minutes | _____ |
| 3 | 30 minutes | _____ |
| 4 | 30 minutes | _____ |
| 5 | 30 minutes | _____ |

| Day | Suggested | Actual |
|---|---|---|
| 6 | Marathon | _____ |
| 7 | optional | _____ |
| Total | 350 minutes | _____ |
| Average | 50 minutes | _____ |

Here are further notes on training for the marathon:

- Choose the marathon you want to run, and then begin the program exactly three months before the race—unless you have averaged less than 30 minutes a day. In that case, review the basic training schedule in chapter 4 before entering this one. If you're running more than 35 minutes a day now, skip all the weeks listing less running than that. There is no reason to back down.

- Run only the one marathon as a serious race this season. If there are other races, treat them lightly and don't let them interfere with training.

- Again, alternate between long and short runs, taking three of each per week with an "optional" day for rest or making up lost training. Short runs amount to about one-tenth of the week's total, long runs make up two-tenths, and the longest runs three-tenths.

- Use your longest weekly run as a "simulation" of the surface, terrain, time of day, and weather conditions you expect to encounter in the race. Practice taking drinks regularly during these runs. Give particular attention to all of this in week 11, when the longest run is 2½ hours.

- Training pace should be similar to your marathon pace—but easier, naturally, because you aren't running nearly as far. Add short "spurts" of faster pace only as a way of keeping your legs lively and loose during long runs.

- This training averages an hour a day for eight weeks (after the initial buildup and before the final week of tapering). Consider it a minimum. Plenty of people have run marathons on this amount. But if you wish to *race* (my definition of racing is doing training pace or faster), you need to obey the "collapse-point" rule: average at least one-third of the race time. If your time will be under three hours, the hour a day is still enough. If it's to be slower than that, add one training minute for each three minutes of racing time.

- I'd better explain a quirk of this schedule. It appears to let faster runners off with less work. They don't, in fact, run less distance, only less time because they cover the required ground faster. One-third of a marathon is about 8½ miles. A three-hour marathoner may do that comfortably in an hour, while a 3½-hour runner may take 70 minutes. But they both work at the same level of effort.

## Splits

The "wall." Marathoners speak of it as if it were a landmark as immovable as the one that crosses China. This wall is part of the mystique of marathoning that implies you aren't truly initiated into the sport until you have come up against this barrier. The "wall" gives rise to the belief that a marathon doesn't really begin until 20 miles. Andrew Crichton, an editor of *Sports Illustrated* who ran marathons, went so far as to write that perhaps the human body just wasn't made to run for more than two hours.

The "wall" by whatever name it goes—"collapse point," "moment of truth," or "the crash"—sounds a lot worse than it feels. I've been to it many times and have no scars to show for the encounter. All I remember feeling when I hit it was a terrible heaviness from the waist down—not true pain, but the sensation that I was dragging an anchor through a swamp. The pace slowed by a minute, usually more, per mile.

My "wall" has never remained at one place and height, as if erected there by the gods. I've come to it as early as 15 miles and as late as 25. Sometimes, it has stopped me dead; at others, it has been no harder to climb than a small hill. A few times, I haven't found it at all.

This experience makes me think several things. First, the "wall" exists, but it isn't a fixed, inevitable feature of marathoning. And we hit it only if we have made a mistake in training or pacing.

You know about training requirements: one-third of the marathon each day, plus regular runs of two-thirds the distance. The reason so many marathoners meet their "wall" at 20 miles of the race is that they stop too often at seven miles or less in training. If you've trained enough, that should knock down half of your "wall." You raze the other half by pacing the marathon wisely. The general principles of pacing are the same here as in all races: run the two halves in about equal time but quite differently in style, like a cautious scientist at first and then as an uninhibited artist.

## Table 14
## Pacing the Marathon

| Total Time | 5 miles | 10 miles | 15 miles | 20 miles | Last 6+ |
|---|---|---|---|---|---|
| 2:30 | 28 min. | 55 min. | 1:22 | 1:52 | 38 min. |
| 2:35 | 29 min. | 57 min. | 1:25 | 1:56 | 39 min. |
| 2:40 | 30 min. | 59 min. | 1:28 | 2:00 | 40 min. |
| 2:45 | 31 min. | 1:01 | 1:31 | 2:04 | 41 min. |
| 2:50 | 32 min. | 1:03 | 1:33 | 2:07 | 43 min. |
| 2:55 | 33 min. | 1:05 | 1:36 | 2:11 | 44 min. |
| 3:00 | 34 min. | 1:07 | 1:39 | 2:15 | 45 min. |
| 3:05 | 35 min. | 1:08 | 1:42 | 2:19 | 46 min. |
| 3:10 | 36 min. | 1:10 | 1:44 | 2:22 | 48 min. |
| 3:15 | 37 min. | 1:12 | 1:47 | 2:26 | 49 min. |
| 3:20 | 38 min. | 1:14 | 1:50 | 2:30 | 50 min. |
| 3:25 | 39 min. | 1:16 | 1:53 | 2:34 | 51 min. |
| 3:30 | 40 min. | 1:18 | 1:55 | 2:37 | 53 min. |
| 3:35 | 41 min. | 1:20 | 1:58 | 2:41 | 54 min. |
| 3:40 | 42 min. | 1:21 | 2:01 | 2:45 | 55 min. |
| 3:45 | 43 min. | 1:23 | 2:04 | 2:49 | 56 min. |
| 3:50 | 44 min. | 1:25 | 2:06 | 2:52 | 58 min. |
| 3:55 | 45 min. | 1:27 | 2:09 | 2:56 | 59 min. |
| 4:00 | 46 min. | 1:29 | 2:12 | 3:00 | 1:00 |
| 4:05 | 47 min. | 1:31 | 2:15 | 3:04 | 1:01 |
| 4:10 | 47 min. | 1:33 | 2:18 | 3:08 | 1:02 |
| 4:15 | 48 min. | 1:34 | 2:20 | 3:11 | 1:04 |
| 4:20 | 49 min. | 1:36 | 2:23 | 3:15 | 1:05 |
| 4:25 | 50 min. | 1:38 | 2:26 | 3:19 | 1:06 |

Note: Select a goal from the total times at left, and then attempt to run the corresponding times at each of the checkpoints. The "splits" are rounded to the nearest minute, so they may vary 30 seconds on either side of the figures indicated.

.The great distance of the marathon multiplies the effects of good and bad pacing. A good pace is one that seems too slow for the first five miles or so. Ideally, you feel like you are just warming up. You do your strongest running in the middle miles, 6 to 20. You then finish as best you can, figuring you may have to slow a little but not letting that happen without a fight.

In studying my best marathons, I've noticed that the first five miles (19 percent of the distance) took 20 percent of the time. In other words, I ran 20 or so seconds per mile *slower* than the overall pace here. Twenty miles to the finish is about 24 percent of the distance, and I used 25 percent of the time to run this—again about 20 seconds a mile slower than even pace. This, of course, meant I had to make up the difference by running faster in the sixth to twentieth miles.

A three-hour marathoner must average 6:52 miles. Using my formula, he'd start and finish with miles of about 7:10, and he'd run about 6:35 in between. I don't expect many of you to heed my warning to start this much slower than marathon pace. So I ask only that you don't let yourself run the first five miles any faster than the overall average. The chart is set for an even-paced start. Think of that as your safe speed limit.

### Self-Test 26
### How Did You Train and Race?

Fill in the training schedule given for this season, or write an adjusted one for yourself. Also, answer these questions as the season goes along:

1. What were your "collapse points" (CPs) by week? (Multiply your average daily amount of running over the past eight weeks by three. The total by the end of the season should exceed your marathon time.)

| Week | CP | Week | CP | Week | CP |
|------|----|------|----|------|----|
| 1 | ___ | 6 | ___ | 11 | ___ |
| 2 | ___ | 7 | ___ | 12 | ___ |
| 3 | ___ | 8 | ___ | 13 | ___ |
| 4 | ___ | 9 | ___ | | |
| 5 | ___ | 10 | ___ | | |

2. How long was your longest run each week? (It should be

two-thirds as long as your predicted marathon time once you reach full training.)

| Week | Longest | Week | Longest | Week | Longest |
|------|---------|------|---------|------|---------|
| 1 | _____ | 6 | _____ | 11 | _____ |
| 2 | _____ | 7 | _____ | 12 | _____ |
| 3 | _____ | 8 | _____ | 13 | _____ |
| 4 | _____ | 9 | _____ | | |
| 5 | | 10 | | | |

3. What was your marathon result?

*Time*      *Pace per Mile*
_____      _____

4. How well did you pace the race? (Estimate the times for each half. Subtract the fast one from the slow. Divide the difference by 26.22 miles. The result should be less than five seconds per mile.)

*Time*      *1st Half*      *2nd Half*      *Sec. per Mile*
_____      _____      _____      _____

5. Did you start too quickly, finish too slowly, or both? (The first five miles should have taken *no less* than 19 percent of the time, and the last 6:22 miles *no more* than 25 percent of the time. Divide those splits by the total time in minutes.)

*First Five Time*      *Percent*      *Last 6.22 Time*      *Percent*

_____      _____      _____      _____
_____      _____      _____      _____
_____      _____      _____      _____
_____      _____      _____      _____

# 27

# Racing Past the Marathon

It was past midnight. The lights in the homes of Rocklin, California, were out. Four other runners were still on the course somewhere, but I couldn't see them, and I had never felt so desperately alone. Nothing I'd ever done seemed quite so senseless as running these laps by myself in the dark after I'd already done so many.

I was trying to run 100 miles. It was an experiment to see how far I could go if I ran for short distances and split them up with sitdown rest breaks, taking most of a day to finish the 100. I ran five miles at a time for the first 50 miles, then 2½-mile intervals. The idea was to avoid letting fatigue accumulate. I had been on this road since noon and now was completing my seventieth mile.

A few cars huddled together in a golf course parking lot. They marked the start and end of each 2½-mile lap, the place where times were taken and the strength was given to go on. But I was beyond help. I sat down for my break and couldn't get back up. The thought of going out into the dark again was too depressing.

I shouted weakly to the scorer, "That's it for me. Write 'DNF' on your sheet."

Another runner, Peter Mattei, was resting in the back of his station wagon. I hadn't seen him until I heard a voice as weak as mine. Peter said, "What do you mean you're quitting? You can't stop now. You only have 30 miles to go!"

He was serious. Compared to the 70 we'd gone and the 100 we had to go, 30 didn't sound like so much. But it was farther than I'd ever gone before this day. It was five or six more hours of running, and at the time, I couldn't face five or six more minutes.

I was very tired *of* running. But to my surprise, I wasn't all that tired *from* running—even after 14½ hours of it. I'd been more tired after all of my marathons. I would have been almost this tired if I'd stayed out at a party until 2:30 a.m.

The next morning, as is my custom after long races, I surveyed the damage. There wasn't much. I wrote in my diary:

"I have no regrets. Everything considered, the long run went amazingly well—twice as far as I'd gone before; ran every step of the 70 miles; the actual running averaged 8:13 a mile; first 50 miles required only 6 3/4 hours when rests were subtracted; no stomach trouble (I'd expected it from trying to mix eating and running); one blister; no severe fatigue; no troublesome stiffness (either during or after)."

The reasons for stopping before the 100 miles ended had little to do with my ability to run on and on. Physically, I'd hit a groove I might have stayed in for twenty-four hours. But mentally, I couldn't handle it.

Later, I saw that I had made three mistakes:

- *I tried 100 miles.* The problem with 100 isn't so much the distance as the time it takes. The race can't help but run into the night—and I don't run gently into the good night. Running in the dark always depresses me, even on short runs. It should have been a distance like 50 miles or 100 kilometers that started and finished in the daylight hours.

- *I ate weirdly.* There wasn't any plan for type, amount, or frequency; I just gobbled impulsively. My diary says I had "30 lemon drops, 12 Vitamin C pills, two Nutraments, two French rolls, a gallon of water, a quart of Gatorade, a quart of apple juice and a bag of pretzels." I should have drunk more (and more often) and eaten less (or nothing).

- *I made the breaks too long*—and stayed too inactive. They totaled almost five hours of rest. This dragged the run out too long, as I sat for one-third of the time. I should have limited the breaks to five or ten minutes and kept walking or stretching in that time.

As it was, though, this run proved to me that Ken Crutchlow and Tom Osler are right in their claims that runner can go a lot farther than they think they can. Crutchlow got me to try that 100. He didn't say, "Do it, Joe." He did something better: he made it sound not only possible but exciting. I interviewed him after he'd run from Los Angeles to San Francisco—550 miles in 10 days. The startling thing about it was that he hadn't trained at all.

"I don't plan these things," the Englishman said. "That's half the fun, going into them unprepared. This is why I can't train. If I had to do this kind of preparation, it would become a bit of a bore. Unlike marathoners who run every day, I don't know my capabilities. I'm always surprising myself with what I'm able to do."

But people don't run fifty-five miles a day on spirit alone. I asked Ken what his technique was for easing the load of miles.

"Five-mile bursts," he said. "That's how I ran it—five miles at a time, with a bit of rest between the runs. I spread the running out over the whole bloody day. Never would have made it otherwise."

What was good enough for untrained Crutchlow seemed good enough for mildly trained me. You already know it didn't work perfectly in the 100. But it worked well enough to show me that stop-and-go running helps runners with average training background run ultra-long distance, as long as they have an uncommon amount of patience.

Tom Osler added supporting evidence for my belief that a runner can immediately double his longest distance if he's not in a hurry. Tom, one of the few Americans ever to run for twenty-four hours, said he "guaranteed" that anyone who can run a marathon can go 50 miles or more without special training. A runner needs only to use two "tricks":

- *Stop often for rest breaks.* Treat the runs as interval sessions, mixing runs of several miles with walks of a few minutes.

- *Drink gallons of heavily sugared mixes.* Osler favors tea, but Coke or juice with extra sugar will do. The drinks provide both the liquid and the energy needed, and at the slow pace of these runs they're absorbed steadily.

Combining the experiences and advice from the three of us, I offer this plan to make you an instant ultramarathoner:

- *Run 50 miles.* This is far enough that it can't be run like a slightly extended marathon (as 50 kilometers can), but not so far that it takes all day and night to run (as 100 miles does). You still may run from dawn to dusk.

- *Don't train for it.* Don't train any longer than you would for a marathon, anyway. Finish a marathon—running all the way at a good pace—before trying 50 miles. Then, train again as you would for the marathon (see chapter 26)—but no more than that. Ignore the previous warnings about "collapse point." Normal distance limits are stretched.

- *Take breaks.* Stop early and often to keep fatigue from mounting. Allow five minutes in every thirty for walking, drinking, stretching, changing clothes, relieving yourself— whatever needs doing. Practice taking these breaks during your longest training run each week, adding an extra half-hour or so to its length to account for the stops.

- *Get help.* Have your own pit person or crew take care of all timing, lap-counting, drink-handling, etc. Reduce your responsibility to the single act of running.

- *Don't fight it.* Forget completely about running against time or against any other runner. The distance is enough of a competitor. Find a gentle pace—neither too fast nor too slow—and eat up the distance in small bites. Concentrate on one thirty-minute bite at a time instead of worrying about the whole 50 miles.

### Self-Test 27
### How Did You Train and Race?

Write a training schedule for the season, imitating the one used for the marathon in chapter 26. Also, answer these questions:

1.  What was your average daily amount of running each week? (Do at least an hour a day for eight weeks, between an initial buildup period and a final tapering week.)

| Week | Average | Week | Average | Week | Average |
|------|---------|------|---------|------|---------|
| 1 | ___ | 6 | ___ | 11 | ___ |
| 2 | ___ | 7 | ___ | 12 | ___ |
| 3 | ___ | 8 | ___ | 13 | ___ |
| 4 | ___ | 9 | ___ | | |
| 5 | ___ | 10 | ___ | | |

2.  How long was your longest run each week? (Do at least two hours when in full training, not including break time.)

| Week | Longest | Week | Longest | Week | Longest |
|------|---------|------|---------|------|---------|
| 1 | ___ | 6 | ___ | 11 | ___ |
| 2 | ___ | 7 | ___ | 12 | ___ |
| 3 | ___ | 8 | ___ | 13 | ___ |
| 4 | ___ | 9 | ___ | | |
| 5 | ___ | 10 | ___ | | |

3.  What was the result of your ultramarathon?

*Distance*                *Time*                *Pace per Mile*

4.  What was your pattern of runs and breaks? (List more than one, and note when the pattern changed if it varied en route.)

*Length of Runs*                *Length of Breaks*

5.  What was your total *running* time, distance, and pace? (Subtract all break time and distance that you walked; estimate if necessary.)

*Time*                *Distance*                *Pace*

___                ___                ___

___                ___                ___

___                ___                ___

___                ___                ___

# Part Four:

# Leaving It

# 28

# Runs Without Ruts

In winter, this not-so-young man's fancy still turns to thoughts of marathoning. By early spring, these thoughts turn into a schedule. Later, just following that schedule turns me into a neurotic.

This is a pattern I know all too well from the other marathon-type work I do: book writing. Winston Churchill described the process best: "Writing a book is an adventure. To begin with, it is a toy, an amusement; then it becomes a mistress, then a master, and finally a tyrant."

I go through a similar evolution every winter and spring as I think of myself as a marathoner again. Each year since 1967 I've gone through the same steps: from excitement, to plan, to committed effort, to neurosis. I think of it as the "Boston Marathon syndrome." It builds slowly in the months before that race, its symptoms growing with the training mileage.

I like the Boston Marathon, of course. It's the thrill of a runner's lifetime, and I've had enough thrills there for several lifetimes. But I don't like some of what it does to me and my running. It gets me wondering and worrying too much:

"Am I running enough? Or too much?"

"Am I eating too much of the wrong things?"

"Is that pain in my Achilles (my knee, my calf, my hamstring, my foot—choose one or more) the one that will end it all?"

"Is that scratchiness behind my nose (that congestion in my chest, that pain in my stomach, etc.) the illness that will leave me in bed on Patriot's Day?"

"Can I hold a sub-seven-minute mile pace in the race if I'm running eight minutes plus in training?"

Instead of running for the present, I train for later. Instead of doing what I want, I do what I think I need and exactly what the schedule says. Instead of anticipating all the things that should go right, I worry about the few that could go wrong. Instead of relaxing and letting good things happen, I strain to make them happen.

Then, the race is run. Whatever happens there, I'm relieved to be back to normal immediately and for most of the next year. Three months of worrying end in three hours, more or less. Then I only worry for runners who are already thinking ahead to their next marathons—the strict schedules they must keep, and the worrying they must keep doing—as they limp away from Boston.

Big races are important as goals to give purpose to many people's running. Training schedules are important as road maps giving directions to the goals. But these maps should be printed with this warning: training for, and racing in, these events may be hazardous to your health, both physical and mental. The hazard is in slipping from routines into ruts.

Some of us have the romantic notion, spawned by writers such as the late coach Percy Cerutty, that we should run as animals do—entirely as we feel, without any preconceived notions about distance and pace. But wild animals don't race marathons or have so many forces urging them *not* to run. Most civilized runners need the discipline, regularity, and security of a pre-set routine. Even after two decades of running, I still need it. But we can't feel we're stuck in a rut from which there's no escape.

Routines are positive and essential, while ruts are negative and destructive. The problem is in recognizing the thin line separating the two, and in learning to stay on the right side of it . . . most of the time, anyway. As my "Boston Marathon syndrome" shows, it's easier for me to advise staying on the healthy side of the line than to do it. It's not much easier for me to define the subtle differences between routines and ruts. But I'll try.

Most people who don't run—and even some of us who do—think that it is boring to run about the same distance, at the

same time, pace, and place each day of the year with no vaca-
tions. But one person's boredom can be another's adventure.
Running is my adventure. Naturally, not every day's run is a
thrill, but all the days together constitute the main form of
excitement in my life. My longest layoff since 1959 has been a
month. I've gone as long as four years without a day off—for
the good reason that I haven't wanted or needed one.

Despite this seemingly unbroken sameness, I've rarely been
bored as a runner because (with a few big exceptions like the
"Boston Marathon syndrome") I've run in ways that make
running a comfortable routine instead of a claustrophobic rut.
The distinction between the two is not found in what is being
done. (On the surface, there's little difference between my
marathon training and the everyday running the rest of the
year.) And it doesn't depend on when or even where. (One of
the least bored runners I know prefers to do most of his running, winter and summer, on an eight-laps-to-the-mile indoor
track.) The distinction between routines and ruts lies in why we
run, how far and how fast it's done, and who is in charge.

**The meaning we give to our runs.** I've read of a psychology
experiment done with children about the age of my daughter.
(I know from living with her that five-year-olds won't do
anything just because they're ordered.) The scientist first told
the kids to make scratches on pieces of paper—random, meaningless marks—until they became tired of it. No child lasted
longer than a few minutes before growing bored and dropping
his pen. Then, the kids were asked to draw pictures of things
that interested them. After an hour of drawing, the researchers
had to ask them to stop.

The children's basic acts were the same in both cases. They
made lines on paper both times. But they kept drawing and
stayed excited only when the drawing had meaning. They made
pictures when they drew, not just marks.

We run because it fits Mark Twain's definition of play: any
activity with great meaning but little purpose. Running is
grownup child's play. This means much more than making
random footprints. It is artwork in the sense that each step adds
to a total picture. As we add new miles, they have to mean
something to the running picture, or else we'll be bored.

**How much and how hard to run.** The way we run is a matter of both distance and pace. Curiously, the people who complain loudest about being bored by running are the ones who run least. There are good reasons for this:

- They don't run far enough to find out how good running can feel. It takes 2-3 miles—15-30 minutes—to get warm and loose, and to start "flowing." Until then, running is a chore. If runners never get that far, it's never more than a chore.

- Either they have not been running long enough or often enough for it ever to be comfortable, or they go so fast that they aren't able to continue long. Either way, such runners are always tired. Chronic fatigue and boredom work together. We seldom enjoy things that tire us excessively, and we seldom tire of things we enjoy.

We all recognize that pace is critical in individual runs and races, but we aren't as aware of long-term pacing. If we hope to run again tomorrow, we have to moderate the natural urge to burn up everything we have today. We must ration our energy over days, not just minutes, if we're to stay out of the fatigue-boredom rut.

**Who is controlling our running?** Relatively few of us have coaches who plan our schedules and see that we carry them out; even fewer have coaches who are little dictators demanding total obedience to commands. But in the way we slavishly follow the plans printed in magazines and books, and those we make up for ourselves, we become our own dictators.

We're our own best friends when we choose our own routines and are sensible about their execution, moving more to the rhythms inside us than to the numbers printed on a page. On the other hand, be become our own worst enemies when we dig ruts and won't step out. We fight ourselves if we try to move in directions and at speeds against our instincts, and we always lose this kind of fight.

I still fall into ruts if I don't watch where I'm going. The schedule *runs me* when I set arbitrary daily quotas for myself, which assume an authority of their own, commanding me to reach them—or else.

Or else what? Is the earth going to open up and swallow me

if I run only 35 minutes today instead of an hour? Who is going to know or care five years from now whether I met my quota or not? In 1984, even I won't know or care. The only thing that will count then is whether I kept running in the years since 1979. Maintaining a flexible routine now is the best assurance that this will happen.

It is important to point toward races and to prepare systematically for them. But it is more important by far that we're all still on our feet long after the racing is over.


### Self-Test 28
### Are You Bogging Down?


1.  Do you insist on matching to the minute the amounts of training ordered by the schedule?

2.  Are you nagged by chronic, low-grade aches and pains that you must not allow to interfere with your program?

3.  Do you frequently get bored with your training but still run your daily quotas?

4.  Do you often find yourself dreading and delaying the start of your runs until you can psych yourself up to them?

5.  Would you stop training as you do if the races didn't require it of you?

6.  Before races, do you magnify every minor physical complaint into a race-threatening crisis?

7.  Have your racing times stopped improving even though you work as hard as ever?

8.  Are your confidence and enthusiasm badly shaken by any racing slump?

9.  After races, are you more likely to complain about what went wrong than to brag about what went right?

10. Have you come to expect better results from yourself than you can produce?

Note: The more times you answer "yes," the more sure you can be that you have raced yourself into rut. If more than half of these questions describe you, ease up on yourself. The training and the racing are running you—rather than vice versa.

# 29

## Child's Play

When I was a child, I thought as a child, played as a child. When I grew up, I gave up childish things—and became an athlete. When I was a child, I played at sport. I played at the sport of the season—in the fall, football; in winter, basketball; in spring, track; in summer, swimming. I played on no team and for no coach. I played in front of no crowds. I played by no rules except those made up on the spot to fit the occasion.

We did keep score, but no one remembered it or cared who won or lost once the game was over. There were no pregame tensions or rituals, and no postgame hostilities or celebrations. We wore no uniforms and took no showers. There was no such word as *training* because we were playing for the day, not to get ready for tomorrow.

Then, I reached the magic and terrible age of 14—high school, time to start thinking of myself as a man, time to quit playing at sports and start working at them. I did what I thought had to be done to be an athlete. I worked with the team, under the coach, and for the crowd. I worked by the rules handed down from higher authorities. I learned that the end result is the important thing in organized sports, and the activity itself is only a means of getting there. You're supposed to help the people in your color of uniform and oppose the ones in the other colors. You must gloat when you beat the other teams and mourn when you lose to them. You have to wash away effort with a shower before going back into the real world. Above all, you must train.

I trained for track for eight years—four in high school, four more in college. The training took me places I couldn't have gone otherwise—to a half-dozen state championships and a couple of state-record times. It took me to a university I wouldn't have attended if I hadn't been a runner, and it paid part of my way. It took me to about a third of the states in the country to run races. And it took me to racing times I couldn't have approached without working so hard and setting aside so much of normal living.

When I was training, I was always fighting with myself. I was straining to pare away tenths of seconds and worrying that my little world would come down on me if I didn't keep improving. I looked at life as if it were bordered by a 440-yard track, and I avoided anything that might prevent my circling that track faster than I had the week before.

Athletes always must progress but never arrive. They have to keep preparing if they are to perform better than they have before. And when that is done, they must strive for something higher yet. They can never be completely satisfied with what they do, because something better always remains to be done.

An athlete can get himself into this corner. The harder he works, the better he becomes, and then the better he must become. So the harder the runner works, the harder he has to work. When he quits wanting to do that work or stops improving, he's finished as a serious athlete.

When I graduated from college, I left the team and heavy competition behind. I had no coach to act as my conscience, no training partners to act as whips in training, and no big races to keep me running scared. I thought then that I'd fallen on bad times in my running, since my mile slowed by half a minute, my two-mile by almost a minute.

But I couldn't quit. There was still something in running that I half-remembered having, but had lost—something I couldn't put into words or numbers, but a memory that somehow had stayed alive through eight years of athletics. I couldn't quit running, so I had to change the way I ran. It wasn't a rational, carefully thought-out change. It was sudden, impulsive, instinctive. One day I was training like an athlete. Midway through an interval workout, I said to myself, "I don't need this any more."

From the next day on, I ran differently—less like an athlete at work and more like a kid at play. A longer, slower, gentler kind of running replaced the harsh stop-and-go of interval work and time-trials.

But changing attitudes wasn't as quick and easy as changing paces. Eight years of training to think like a jock couldn't be turned around in a few days—not even in a few years. The long-standing habits that had served me well as an athlete stood in the way of true fun-running.

For an athlete who thinks of his career as a mountain climb—always going uphill, always pushing for higher ground—backing down is hard. It's hard when such a runner is forced to accept a permanent place at a lower level.

For several years, after I left serious competition, I had trouble accepting being outrun by people I had beaten before and could beat again if I worked a little harder. I was tempted to up my mileage and pace again—until I remembered racing success required that I think and train like an athlete. But I wasn't an athlete anymore. I'm not criticizing athletes and what they stand for. I'm proud to have been one and to have done what I did. I'll fight anyone who says my 4:18 mile doesn't mean anything. I carry no regrets and no bitterness about the work I had to do to run this well.

But that is in the past. I've decided to run for the rest of my life instead of for next week's race. So my running has to be more like child's play and less like the work it was when I was a serious athlete.

### Self-Test 29

### How Athletic Are You?

1. Is preparing for races your most important reason for running every day?

2. Do you intentionally make your training hurt so you can tolerate pain in races?

3. Are you a high goal-setter who believes a person's ability is limited mainly by his imagination?

4.  Do you give up foods and drinks you like just so you can run farther or faster?

5.  Do your athletic practices appear abnormal compared to the habits of your family and friends?

6.  Do you train with a group or team so you can run farther or faster than you would alone?

7.  Is it important to you that you beat certain people or place a certain way in competition?

8.  Are you always asking yourself to go a little faster, a little farther?

9.  Are you always comparing your current performances with past marks and expecting them to progress?

10. Do you think you must always stay a little bit dissatisfied with yourself so you'll keep trying to improve?


Note: A true athlete would answer "yes" to most, if not all, of these questions.

# 30

# Ten Commandments

When I became an athlete, I learned and accepted without question a code of conduct that ran something like this:

1. Train hard.
2. Attack the barriers of pain.
3. Set high goals; reach for the stars.
4. Live a pure life and think clean thoughts by following a rigid set of training rules.
5. Make sacrifices in order to succeed; temporarily set aside normal living.
6. Work as a team so the group will be stronger than the sum of its parts.
7. Run to win, and take anything less than victory as a personal insult.
8. Keep pushing the pace; you can always go faster than you think you can.
9. Keep trying to raise your own standards of performance and your expectations.
10. Pursue excellence; seek perfection.

When I quit trying to be an athlete and began running for fun, I had to play by different rules. The athlete and the fun-runner are different, both in the way they think and the way they act. Athletes can occasionally back off and run just for fun. Fun-runners can get serious and race well. But their basic outlooks and routines are very different.

An athlete must always be vaguely dissatisfied with who he is and what he has done. This drives him to do the work needed to become a better competitor. He doesn't accept and adjust to things as they are; he fights the status quo.

A fun-runner, on the other hand, must learn to be happy with himself most of the time. He has few things to prove through his running. It is, in George Sheehan's words, "not a test but a therapy, not a question but an answer." It is more a comfort than a challenge, and it brings more pleasure than pain. The fun-runner runs to renew the pleasure. Every day isn't as much fun as every other, but the good ones are never as far away as the successes the athlete is chasing.

The "Ten Commandments of Fun-Running" oppose almost exactly those I worked under as an athlete. You won't see these posted on locker room walls:

1. **Drop the word** *train* **from your vocabulary.** At least, the word *train* should not apply to the kind of running you're doing. This may seem a small matter, but it involves more than semantics. To think of running as "training" implies that it is important only for what it might give you tomorrow. Today's running is thought of merely as preparation for the big event. Instead of "training," run for today. If you take care of today, tomorrow will take care of itself.

2. **Accept pain as a friend.** Recognize it as the boundary line within which you can run safely. Discomfort and pain need not be ignored, feared, or challenged the way an athlete must treat them. They can be early warnings of approaching trouble, gentle reminders that you should back off before the big trouble arrives.

3. **Think small.** Learn to take pleasure in common, everyday sights, and thoughts and actions. Learn that the biggest victory you can achieve is to have the desire, and be able, to run each day.

4. **Be flexible.** Set no rules so rigid that they can't have exceptions or be modified. Run like the water, which adapts to changing circumstances, instead of running like a rolling stone, which yields to nothing in its path. Remember that in time the water can wear down the stone.

**5. Live normally.** Fit running in among the day's activities instead of doing things the other way around. Running is most likely to last if it is as normal and natural a part of each day as eating breakfast and reading the newspaper. It will last if it is a daily plus instead of a minus.

**6. Be something of a loner.** Beware of organizations, because getting involved with them quickly drains the playful spontaneity out of running. One of the best reasons to run is to escape the group structures and rules that limit most of our movements. One of the real pleasures is the chance to be alone.

**7. Redefine victory.** To the fun-runner, *winning* is the ability and desire to keep going, to endure. *Victory* is measured not in tenths of seconds or places on a results sheet, but simply by staying in the running.

**8. Slow down.** Pace yourself for a long career, the way a marathoner paces himself for his race. To run seven-minute miles for 26-plus miles, a marathoner can't race the first mile in 4:30. A year for a lifetime runner is like a mile for a marathoner. Hold down the pace this year if you want to finish a career lasting decades.

**9. Don't compare.** Appreciate what you might have done before as a serious runner, but don't constantly compare your present performance with your old abilities. If you always need to be faster than you were before, this will cut short your running life; everyone must slow down sometime.

**10. Accept imperfection.** The pursuit of excellence breeds frustration, because no matter how good you get, you feel you could do a little more, a little better. Don't always be asking yourself, "But what if . . . ?" Do what you can with what you have, and be as happy with the running itself as with the results.

### Self-Test 30

### Are You a Fun-Runner?

1. Have you started thinking of your daily runs not as "training" but as pleasant ends in themselves?

2.  If you still keep a running diary at all, is a time within five minutes, or a distance within a mile, accurate enough?

3.  Do you run more by how you feel than by a detailed plan?

4.  Can you take time out in mid-run, stop early, or even skip a day without feeling guilty about it?

5.  However, when you must miss all or a part of a run, do you feel like an old friend has left you for awhile?

6.  Would you keep running as you do now even if you never race?

7.  Do you often decide whether to race when you wake the day of a race?

8.  Do you race without planning your pace?

9.  Can you "run through" a race at an easy pace and still feel good about the experience?

10. Are you proud of your older, faster times—but not so haunted by them that you can't appreciate a race a minute per mile slower?

Note: The more "yes" answers you give, the more likely that you have evolved to the highest level of running—that is, you have raced until you don't need racing anymore. This book was meant to help take you there.

# Appendix

# Racing Distances

## ENGLISH

| Race | Conversion |
|---|---|
| 1 mile | 1,609 meters |
| 2 miles | 3,219 meters |
| 3 miles | 4,828 meters |
| 5 miles | 8,047 meters |
| 6 miles | 9,656 meters |
| 10 miles | 16,193 meters |
| Half-marathon | 21,098 meters |
| 15 miles | 24,140 meters |
| 20 miles | 32,187 meters |
| Marathon | 42,195 meters |
| 30 miles | 48,280 meters |
| 50 miles | 80,467 meters |

## METRIC

| Race | Conversion |
|---|---|
| 1,500 meters | 0.93 miles |
| 3,000 meters | 1.86 miles |
| 5,000 meters | 3.11 miles |
| 8,000 meters | 4.97 miles |
| 10,000 meters | 6.21 miles |
| 15,000 meters | 9.32 miles |
| 20,000 meters | 12.43 miles |
| 25,000 meters | 15.53 miles |
| 30,000 meters | 18.64 miles |
| Marathon | 26.22 miles |
| 50,000 meters | 31.07 miles |
| 100,000 meters | 62.14 miles |

Note: The English events and the metric ones beside them are the standard races, and are comparable in distance. Exact English-to-metric and metric-to-English conversions are given. (A kilometer is 1,000 meters, which converts to 1,093 yards or 0.62 mile.)

# Racing Information

More than a dozen national and regional magazines publish current race schedules and results, plus feature articles on training and racing. The leading publications available in late-1978 are:

- *Harrier:* Mike Muska, editor, Box 1550, Auburn, Al 36830; specializing in cross-country; published every two weeks during that season, and once in spring and summer.
- *Marathoner:* Bob Anderson, publisher, Box 366, Mountain View, CA 94042; specializing in marathoning and ultra-marathoning; published four times a year.
- *NorCal Running Review:* Jack Leydig, editor, Box 1551, San Mateo, CA 94401; West Coast, with emphasis on Northern California; published six times a year.
- *On the Run:* Bob Anderson, editor, Box 366, Mountain View, CA 94042; published twice a month.
- *Runner:* Jonathan Larsen, editor, 1 Park Avenue, New York, NY 10016; published monthly.
- *Runner's Gazette:* Ed Gildea, editor, 102 Water Street, Lansford, PA 19232; emphasis on northeastern U.S.; published every other month.
- *Runner's World:* Bob Anderson, editor, Box 366, Mountain View, CA 94042; published monthly.
- *Running:* E. C. Frederick, editor, Box 350, Salem, OR 97308; published four times a year.
- *Running Review:* Lloyd Peters, editor, 645 S. Prince St., Lancaster, PA 17603; published monthly.
- *Stride On:* Hal Higdon, editor, Box 372, Michigan City, IN 46360; covering the Midwest; published four times a year.
- *Running Times:* Edward Ayres, editor, 12808 Occoquan Rd., Woodbridge, VA 22192; published monthly.
- *Track & Field News:* Bert Nelson, editor, Box 296, Los Altos, CA 94022; published monthly.
- *Yankee Runner:* Rick Bayko, editor, 19 Grove St., Merrimac, MA 01860; covering New England; published 18 times a year.

# AAU Programs

The Amateur Athletic Union (AAU) oversees most of the country's long-distance races. More than fifty regional "associations" make up the National AAU. Some states have more than one association, while some associations cross state lines. Listed here are the AAU long-distance running chairmen by state. They are sources of registration, race schedules, and club information. The national chairman is Bob Campbell, 39 Linnet St., West Roxbury, MA 02132.

## ALABAMA

*Southeastern AAU* — Harold Canfield, 502 Alandale Rd., Knoxville, TN 37920

## ALASKA

*Alaska AAU* — Terry Martin, 3960 Reka Dr., Anchorage, AK 99504

## ARIZONA

*Arizona AAU* — Gus Armstrong, 6112 N. 17th Ave., Phoenix, AZ 85015

## ARKANSAS

*Arkansas AAU* — Terry Mathews, 2200 Worthen Bank Bldg., Little Rock, AK 72201

## CALIFORNIA

*Central California AAU* — David Bronzan, Box 271, Fresno, CA 93708

*Pacific AAU* — Roger Bryan, 950 E. Hillsdale, No. 210, Foster City, CA 94404

*Pacific Southwest AAU* — Will Rasmussen, 1542 Hillsmont Dr., El Cajon, CA 92020

*Southern Pacific AAU* — John Duhig, 1642 Trafalgar Pl., Westlake Village, CA 91361

## COLORADO

*Rocky Mountain AAU* — Ben Magsameri, 1200 E. Elizabeth, Ft. Collins, CO 80521

## CONNECTICUT

*Connecticut AAU* – Vin Fandetti, 100 Oxboro Dr., No. C-1, Glastonbury, CT 06033

## DELAWARE

*South Atlantic AAU* – George Adams, 1001 Bernadette Dr., Forest Hill, MD 21050

## DISTRICT OF COLUMBIA

*Potomac Valley AAU* – Rich Good, 1521 Eastbound Dr., Silver Spring, MD 20904

## FLORIDA

*Florida AAU* – Max Clark, 433 N. Mills Ave., Orlando, FL 32803

*Florida Gold Coast AAU* – George Zell, 13752 S.W. 48th St., Miami, FL 33175

## GEORGIA

*Georgia AAU* – Dave Martin, Georgia State University, University Plaza, Atlanta, GA 30303

## HAWAII

*Hawaiian AAU* – Jim Moberly, 44-122 Kalenarai Pl., Kaneohe, HI 96744

## IDAHO

*Inland Empire AAU* – Dave Haugen, 808 Summit Dr., Cheney, WA 99004

*Intermountain AAU* – Ben Peterson, 1054 E. 8600 S., Sandy, UT 84070

## ILLINOIS

*Central AAU* – Richard King, 5600 S. Drexel Ave., Chicago, IL 60637

*Ozark AAU* – Charles Lewis, 2075 Gerard Pk., Florissant, MO 63033

## INDIANA

*Indiana AAU* – Steve Jones, 3959 Central Ave., Indianapolis, IN 46205

## IOWA

*Iowa AAU* – Bob Hunerdosse, 901 N. 10th, Fairfield, IA 52556

*Midwestern AAU* – Greg Carlberg, 2011 N. 54th, Omaha, NE 68104

## KANSAS

*Missouri Valley AAU* – Carl Owczarzak, 6823 W. 77th Terr., Overland Park, KS 66204

## KENTUCKY

*Kentucky AAU* – Charles Ziporich, 9616 Elm Lake Dr., Louisville, KY 40291

## LOUISIANA

*Southern AAU* – Dr. J. Dorok, 723 Seyburn Ct., Baton Rouge, LA 70808

## MAINE

*Maine AAU* – Harold Paulson, Box 8046, Portland, ME 04104

## MARYLAND

*Potomac Valley AAU* – Rich Good, 1521 Eastbound Dr., Silver Spring, MD 20904

*South Atlantic AAU* – George Adams, 1001 Bernadette Dr., Forest Hill, MD 21050

## MASSACHUSETTS

*New England AAU* – Fred Brown, 157 Walsh St., Medford, MA 02155

## MICHIGAN

*Michigan AAU* – Edward Kozloff, 10144 Lincoln, Huntington Woods, MI 48070

## MINNESOTA

*Minnesota AAU* – Ed Arenz, 4094 Flowerfield Rd., St. Paul, MN 55112

## MISSISSIPPI

*Southern AAU* – Dr. J. Dorok, 723 Seyburn Ct., Baton Rouge, LA 70808

## MISSOURI

*Missouri Valley AAU* — Carl Owczarzak, 6823 W. 77th Terr., Overland Park, KA 66204

*Ozark AAU* — Charles Lewis, 2075 Gerard Pk., Florissant, MO 63033

## MONTANA

*Montana AAU* — Dave Pidcock, 405–27th Ave., N.E., Great Falls, MT 59404

## NEBRASKA

*Midwestern AAU* — Greg Carlberg, 2011 N. 54th, Omaha, NE 68104

## NEVADA

*Pacific AAU* — Roger Bryan, 950 E. Hillsdale, No. 210, Foster City, CA 94404

*Southern Nevada AAU* — Laura Jean Miller, 106 Lake Meade Dr., No. 107, Henderson, NV 89015

## NEW HAMPSHIRE

*New England AAU* — Fred Brown, 157 Walsh St., Medford, MA 02155

## NEW JERSEY

*Middle Atlantic AAU* — Joseph McIlhinney, 7508 Fourth Ave., Melrose Park, PA 19126

*New Jersey AAU* — Harry Henriquez, 26 Ellis Dr., Basking Ridge, NJ 07920

## NEW MEXICO

*New Mexico AAU* — Michael Danoff, 5417 Rawling Rd., N.E., Albuquerque, NM 87111

## NEW YORK

*Adirondack AAU* — William Shrader, RFD 1, Middleburg, NY 12122

*Metropolitan AAU* — Ken Abramson, 138-10 Franklin Ave., Flushing, NY 11355

*Niagara AAU* — Richard Kendall, 41 Grayton Rd., Tonwanda, NY 14150

## NORTH CAROLINA

*North Carolina AAU* — Don Jayroe, 602 Wimbledon Dr., Raleigh, NC 27609

## NORTH DAKOTA

*North Dakota AAU* — Lyle Kitchen, 2 Woodland Dr., Fargo, ND 58701

## OHIO

*Lake Erie AAU* — James Klett, 311 Perdue St., Akron, OH 44310

*Ohio AAU* — Felix LeBlanc, 4508 Keeler Dr., Columbus, OH 43227

## OKLAHOMA

*Oklahoma AAU* — Rob Doenges, 5395–27th Pl., Tulsa, OK 74114

## OREGON

*Oregon AAU* — John Frey, 1450 Fir St., Salem, OR 97302

## PENNSYLVANIA

*Allegheny Mountain AAU* — Mel Albright, 415 Wirsing Ave., Greensburg, PA 15601

*Middle Atlantic AAU* — Joseph McIlhinney, 7508 Fourth Ave., Melrose Park, PA 19126

## RHODE ISLAND

*New England AAU* — Fred Brown, 157 Walsh St., Medford, MA 02155

## SOUTH CAROLINA

*South Carolina AAU* — Michael Mauldin, Box 1537, Columbia, SC 29202

## SOUTH DAKOTA

*South Dakota AAU* — Al Birkholz, 3308 Grandview Dr., Rapid City, SD 57701

## TENNESSEE

*Southeastern AAU* — Harold Canfield, 502 Alandale Rd., Knoxville, TN 37920

**TEXAS**

*Border AAU* — Allen Veach, 5119 Garry Owen, El Paso, TX 79903

*Gulf AAU* — George Kleeman, 227 Faust, Houston, TX 77024

*South Texas* — Howard Johnson, 523 Cave Lane, San Antonio, TX 78233

*Southwestern* — Will Samples, 3401 St. Johns Dr., Dallas, TX 75205

*West Texas* — Dick Walker, Box 2000, Lubbock, TX 79457

**UTAH**

*Intermountain AAU* — Ben Peterson, 1054 E. 8600 S., Sandy, UT 84070

**VERMONT**

*New England AAU* — Fred Brown, 157 Walsh St., Medford, MA 02155

**VIRGINIA**

*Potomac Valley AAU* — Rich Good, 1521 Eastbound Dr., Silver Spring, MD 20904

*Virginia AAU* — Charlie George, 801 Yearling Ct., Virginia Beach, VA 23462

**WASHINGTON**

*Inland Empire AAU* — Dave Haugen, 808 Summit Dr., Cheney, WA 99004

*Pacific Northwest AAU* — Laurel James, 7210 E. Green Lake Dr., N., Seattle, WA 98103

**WEST VIRGINIA**

*West Virginia AAU* — Carl Hatfield, Box 1397, A-B College, Philippi, WV 26416

**WISCONSIN**

*Wisconsin AAU* — John Tierney, 4628 N. Idlewood Ave., Milwaukee, WI 53211

**WYOMING**

*Wyoming AAU* — Brent Weigner, 2722 Van Lennen, Cheyenne, WY 82001

# RRC Programs

Road Runners Clubs serve more than 50,000 racers in 175 chapters spread through most of the states. Listed here are the affiliates of the R.R.C. of America, led by Jeff Darman, 2737 Devonshire Place, N.W., Washington, DC 20008. Contact Darman for information on forming a club. Write to the nearest club for details on its program.

## ALABAMA

*Birmingham T. C.* Versal Spalding, 2405 Henrietta Rd. Ct., Birmingham, AL 35223

*Central Alabama R.R.C.* Jeff Magnin, 4342 White Acres Rd., Montgomery, AL 36106

*Coosa Valley T.C.* Tony Stepleton, Box 602, Anniston, AL 36201

*Huntsville T.C.* Harold Tinsley Sr., 8811 Edgehill Dr., S.E., Huntsville, AL 35802

*Troy T.C.* Nick Costes, Troy State University, Troy, AL 36081

*Wiregrass R.R.C.* Larry Nolen, 35 Richardson Dr., Daleville, AL 36322

## ARIZONA

*Arizona R.R.C.* Charles Rice, 10055 E. Cactus Rd., Scottsdale, AZ 85260

*Southern Arizona R.R.C.* Joseph Cary, 25 Foldfinch Circle, Sierra Vista, AZ 85635

## ARKANSAS

*Little Rock Hash House Harriers* Bill Brass, 1503 Johnson St., Jacksonville, AK 72076

*Little Rock R.R.C.* Lloyd Walker, 1516 War Eagle Dr., North Little Rock, AK 72116

## CALIFORNIA

*Bay Area R.R.C.* Robert Wright, 29 Greenwood Way, Monterey, CA 93940

*Club Northridge* Charlie Horn, 714 Acacia Ave., Glendale, CA 91205

*East Bay R.R.C.* Gail Wetzork, 1940 Webster St., Oakland, CA 94612

*Empire Runners* Glenn McCarthy, 335 Algiers Ct., Santa Rosa, CA 95405

*Half Moon Bay Coasters R.C.* Bill Hunja, 637 Buena Vista St., Moss Beach, CA 94038

*Lake Merritt Joggers & Striders* John Notch, 230 Marlow Dr., Oakland, CA 94605

*San Francisco D.S.E. Runners* Walt Stack, 321 Collingwood, San Francisco, CA 94114

*San Luis D.C.* Stan Rosenfield, Box 1134, San Luis Obispo, CA 93406

*Sierra Slowpokes R.C.* Gary Loucks, 116 High St., Grass Valley, CA 95945

*Valley of the Moon R.C.* Dave Sjostedt, Box 562, Bodega Bay, CA 94923

**COLORADO**

*Aspen T. C.* Bob Forque, Box 8215, Aspen, CO 81611

*Border Runners* T. V. Hagenah, 214 Chestnut, Trinidad, CO 81082

*Colorado T.C.* Dave Peters, 1317 Seventh, Boulder, CO 80302

*Colorado Masters R.A.* Bill & Nancy Hamaker, 1525 S. Lansing St., Aurora, CO 80012

*Denver T.C.* Steve Kaeuper, 2263 Kameria, Denver, CO 80207

*Ft. Collins T.C.* Rich Sadowske, 821 W. Myrtle, Ft. Collins, CO 80521

*Mesa Monument Striders* Clarence Craig, 2502 First St., Grand Junction, CO 81501

*Northern Colorado T.C.* Doug Bell, 1524 11th St., Greeley, CO 80631

*Pike's Peak R.R.C.* Carl McDaniel, 3360 Red Onion Cir., Colorado Springs, CO 80918

*Rocky Mountain R.R.C.* Buzz Yancey, 929 Washington No. 5, Denver, CO 80203

*San Juan Mountain Runners* Tom Haggard, Route 1, Box 221, Montrose, CO 81401

*Timber Ridge Runners* Gary Phippen, Box 162, Evergreen, CO 80439

**CONNECTICUT**

*Hartford T.C.* Vin Fandetti, 100 Oxbow Dr., C-1, Glastonbury, CT 06033

**FLORIDA**

*Boca Raton R.R.C.* Jon Campbell, Box 680, Boca Raton, FL 33432

*Ft. Lauderdale R.R.C.* Lynn Tunks, 831 N.E. 60th St., Ft. Lauderdale, FL 33334

*Florida T.C.* Lenny Rhine, Box 12463, University Station, Gainesville, FL 32604

*Gulf Winds T.C.* Dr. James Penrod, 2412 Winthrop Rd., Tallahassee, FL 32303

*Jacksonville T.C.* John Fannin, Box 515, Jacksonville, FL 32201

*Miami Runners* Hans Huseby, 6450 S.W. 82 St., South Miami, FL 33143

*Northwest Florida T.C.* Ed Sears, 174 Charles Dr., Valparaiso, FL 32580

*Pensacola Runners Assn.* Stuart Towns, Box 2691, Pensacola, FL 32503

*Suncoast Runners* Tom White, 1250 Jungle Ave., St. Petersburg, FL 33710

*Valparaiso-Niceville A.A.* Fred Carley, 2648 Edgewater Dr., Niceville, FL 32578

**GEORGIA**

*Emerald City R.R.C.* Dr. J. Y. Jones, 209 Earlwood Dr., Dublin, GA 31021

*Savannah Striders* Dr. Cedric Stratton, 506 E. 57th St., Savannah, GA 31405

*West Georgia T.C.* Doug Vassy, 401 Tanner St., Carrollton, GA 30117

**HAWAII**

*Mid-Pacific R.R.C.* Gordon Dugan, 704 Ainapo, Honolulu, HI 96825

## IDAHO

*Blackfoot R.R.C.* Dean Packham, 288½ N. Shilling Ave., Blackfoot, ID 83221

## IOWA

*Cornbelt R.C.* Karl Urgurean, 203-E. Denisen, Davenport, IA 52804

## ILLINOIS

*Club North Shore* Cynthia McKenzie, 643 Euclid, Highland Park, IL 60035

*Galesburg R.R.C.* Evan Massey, 1080 Tamarind, Galesburg, IL 61401

*Glenview R.R.C.* Jerry Parsons, 1504 Pfingsten Rd., Glenview, IL 60025

*Illinois R.R.C.* Joe O'Shea, Box 2976, Station A, Champaign, IL 61820

*Illinois Valley Striders* Steven Shostrom, 3018 N. Bigelow, Peoria, IL 61604

*Midwest R.R.C.* Dick King, 5600 S. Drexel, Chicago, IL 60606

*Moraine T.C.* Mike Beard, 6826 Chelsea Rd., Tinley Park, IL 60477

*Springfield R.R.C.* Phil Peterson, 2505 Churchill Rd., Springfield, IL 62702

## INDIANA

*Ft. Wayne T.C.* Charlie Brandt, 5334 Moon Rock Ct., Ft. Wayne, IN 46804

*Hoosier R.R.C.* Chuck Koeppen, 1815 E. 117th St., Carmel, IN 46032

## KANSAS

*Mid-American Masters* Bob Creighton, 111 S. Sixth St., Atwood, KS 67730

*Wichita R.C.* Brent Wooten, 3054 S. Custer, Wichita, KS 67217

## KENTUCKY

*Blue Grass R.R.C.* Jerry Stone, Route 3, Georgetown, KY 40324

*Paducah R.R.C.* William Hayden, Rt. 1, Box 121, Paducah, KY 42001

## LOUISIANA

*Bogalusa Striders* John McIntire, 1127 N. Borden Dr., Bogalusa, LA 70427

*Club South Runners* John Jumonville, Box 65123, Baton Rouge, LA 70896

*New Orleans T.C.* President, Box 30491, New Orleans, LA 70190

*R.R.C. of Slidell* Ray Durham, 675 Dale Ave., Slidell, LA 70458

## MAINE

*Central Maine Striders* Fred Judkins, 35 Boutelle Ave., Waterville, ME 04901

## MARYLAND

*Baltimore R.R.C.* John Roemer, Rt. 1, Box 246, Evna Rd., Parkton, MD 21120

*Frederick Steeplechasers* Bert Coursey, 8607 Imagination Ct., Walkerville, MD 21793

*Queen City Striders* Ray Kiddy, 1916 Harrow Ln., Cumberland, MD 21502

*RASAC* Joseph Lacetera, 1006 Whitaker Mill Rd., Joppa, MD 21085

*Sea Gull R.R.C.* Dr. Bob McBrien, 301 New York Ave., Salisbury, MD 21801

*Upper Montgomery County R.R.C.* Ray McInerney, 567 Summit Hall Rd., Gaithersburg, MD 20760

*Westminster Area R.R.C.* Donald Myers, 23 Kalten Rd., Westminister, MD 21157

## MASSACHUSETTS

*Berkshire Hill Runners* Jim Dami, 17 Frederick St., North Adams, MA 01247

*Central Mass. Striders* Wayne Lamothe, 9 Atwood Rd., Cherry Valley, MA 01611

*Greater Springfield Harriers* Peter Stasz, 120 Longhill St., No. 7, Springfield, MA 01108

*Mohawk Trail Runners* Tony Gutierrez, 36th Medical Battalion, Ft. Devans, MA 01433

*Nantucket Easy Striders T.C.* David Hetherman, 67 Center St., Nantucket, MA 02554

*New England R.R.C.* Rick Bayko, 19 Grove St., Merrimac, MA 01860

*Poet's Seat Ridge Runners* Edward Porter, 26 Madison Cir., Greenfield, MA 01301

*Sharon R.R.C.* Dale Van Meter, 66 Summit Ave., Sharon, MA 02067

*Sugarloaf Mountain A.C.* Don Grant, Box 659, Amherst, MA 01966

*Wingaersheek Runners* Donald Spittle, 203 South St., Rockport, MA 01966

## MICHIGAN

*Battle Creek R.R.C.* Roger Larsen, 157 Orchard, Battle Creek, MI 49017

*Kalamazoo T.C.* Tom Doxey, 5632 Roanoke, Portage, MI 49081

*Mid-Michigan T.C.* Bill Keller, 2718 Wabash, Lansing, MI 48910

*North Berrien Striders* Jerry Ingram, 2522 S. State, St. Joseph, MI 49085

*Saginaw T.C.* Ray Bartels, 440 Winfield, Saginaw, MI 48603

*Upper Peninsula R.R.C.* Bob Olson, 1054 N. Lincoln Rd., Hancock, MI 49930

## MINNESOTA

*Minnesota Distance Running Assn.* Box 14064, University Station, Minneapolis, MN 55414

## MISSISSIPPI

*Hattiesburg T.C.,* John Pendergrass, Box 1203, Hattiesburg, MS 39401

*Mississippi T.C.* Walter Howell, 608 Dunton Rd., Clinton, MS 39056

*Mississippi Gulf Coast J.C.* Terry Delcuze, Box 4010, Biloxi, MS 39531

*Possum Town Trotters* Robbie Robinson, Rt. 1, West Woods II, West Point, MS 39773

## MISSOURI

*Columbia T.C.* Joe Duncan, 2980 Maple Bluff Dr., Columbia, MO 65201

*Ozark Mountain Ridge Runners* Clyde Johnson, 847 N. Lone Pine St., Springfield, MO 65802

*St. Louis T.C.* Jerry Kokesh, 1226 Orchard Village Dr., Manchester, MO 63011

**MONTANA**

*Big Sky Wind Drinkers* Andy Blank, Box 1766, Bozeman, MT 59715

**NEBRASKA**

*Lincoln T.C.* Jim Lewis, 2900 John Ave., Lincoln, NB 68502

*Plains T.C.* Dick McMahon, 4561 Charles, Omaha, NB 68132

*Scottsbluff Striders* David Challed, 1724 Second Ave., Scottsbluff, NB 69361

**NEVADA**

*Las Vegas T.C.* Tony Gerardi, 5020 Lancaster Dr., Las Vegas, NV 89120

**NEW HAMPSHIRE**

*Manchester Y R.C.* Tom Wallace, 123 Smyth Rd., Manchester, NH 03101

**NEW JERSEY**

*Central Jersey R.R.C.* Harry Brown, 208 Greenbrook Rd., Greenbrook, NJ 08812

**NEW YORK**

*Greater Rochester T.C.* Paul Gesell, 4472 Main St., Hemlock, NY 14466

*Hudson-Mohawk R.R.C.* Bill Meehan, 16 Kramer Rd., Guilderland, NY 12084

*New York R.R.C.* Fred Lebow, Box 881 FDR Station, New York, NY 10022

*Northport R.C.* David Harris, Box 554, Northport, NY 11768

*Rockland R.R.C.* Ellen Fostoff, Box 308, New City, NY 10956

*Suburban R.R.C.* Steve Marek, Box 294, Millwood, NY 10546

*Tatonic R.R.C.* Daniel Caffery, Box 99, Baldwin Place, NY 10505

*Triple Cities R.C.* Alan Jones, 3717 Wildwood Dr., Endwell, NY 13760

*Utica YMCA R.R.C.* Robert Carlson, 726 Washington St., Utica, NY 13502

## NORTH CAROLINA

*Asheville T.C.* Charlie Baker, 47 Mountainbrook Rd., Asheville, NC 28805

*Carolina Godiva T.C.* Walter High, Box 16, Carolina Union, UNC-CH, Chapel Hill, NC 27514

*Charlotte-Mechlenburg T.C.* Gary Church, Two NCNB Plaza, Charlotte, NC 28280

*Coastal Carolina T.C.* Bob Morrison, Box 3045, Greenville, NC 27834

*Cumberland County R.R.C.* Jeff Blount, 419 Curbrain Ct., Fayetteville, NC 28304

*Twin City T.C.* Jon Lewis, 826 Austin Ln., Winston-Salem, NC 27106

## NEW MEXICO

*Atomic City* John Cappis, 30 Glenview Ct., Los Alamos, NM 87544

## OHIO

*Cleveland West R.R.C.* William Reidy, 3491 Beverly Hills Rd., Rocky River, OH 44116

*Lima Run and Jog Club* Jon Pauff, 5399 Sandusky Rd., Lima, OH 45801

*Ohio River R.R.C.* Felix LeBlanc, 1013 Tralee Trail, Dayton, OH 45430

*Southeast R.C.* Reno Starnoni, 878 Wellmon, Bedford, OH 44146

*Toledo R.R.C.* Tom Kovacs, 3262 N. Beach Dr., Oregon, OH 43616

*Youngstown R.R.C.* Don Smaltz, 4678 Burkey Rd., Youngstown, OH 44515

## OREGON

*Oregon R.R.C.* Ken Weidcamp, Box D. Beaverton, OR 97005

## PENNSYLVANIA

*Allegheny Mountain R.R.C.* Shirley McDanials, 721 Vallevista Ave., Pittsburgh, PA 15234

*Central Susquehana R.R.C.* James Dolan, Rt. 2, Box 150, Lock Haven, PA 17745

*Chambersburg R.R.C.* Chuck Lesher, Rt. 10, Box 38, Chambersburg, PA 17201

*Delco Joggers* Byron Munday, 214 Blunston, Collingdale, PA 19023

*Greater Pittsburgh R.R.C.* Skip Brown, Kimberly Estates, Rt. 3, Box 497-J, Mt. Pleasant, PA 15666

*Harrisburg Area R.R.C.* Paul Hurley Jr., 28 South 29th St., Camp Hill, PA 17011

*Lancaster R.R.C.* Earl Furman, 2727 Columbia Ave., Lancaster, PA 17603

*Mid-Atlantic R.R.C.* Cris Tatreau, Memoria Hall, West Park, Philadelphia, PA 19131

*Octoraraa R.C.* Rev. Robert Kopp, 518 W. Main St., Parkesburg, PA 19365

*Reading R.R.C.* Bruce Zeidman, 211 N.Sixth St., Reading, PA 19601

*Sudbury R.R.C.* Robert Hiffert, 26 Cataivissa Ave., Sudbury, PA 17801

*Valley Forge R.R.C.* Rev. Raymond Reighn, Pawling Rd., Phonixville, PA 19460

*Windsor T.C.* Todd Howard, 126 W. Main St., Windsor, PA 17366

*Wizz Kids* Rt. 2, Orangeville, PA 17857

## SOUTH CAROLINA

*Greenville T.C.* Adrian Craven, Rt. 9, Woodhaven Dr., Greenville, SC 29609

*Lancaster R.C.* Claude Sinclair Jr., 412 Williams Cir., Lancaster, SC 29720

*Myrtle Beach R.R.C.* Sean Ryan, 4102 North Kings Highway, Myrtle Beach, SC 29577

## TENNESSEE

*Chattanooga T.C.* Jerry Grahn, Athletic Attic, Eastgate Mall, Chattanooga, TN 37411

*Eagle U. R.C.* Gerald Koch, 101 Lacy Ln., Clarksville, TN 37040

*State of Franklin T.C.* Rick Earnest, 4109 Lindenwood, Kingsport, TN 37663

## TEXAS

*Alief R.R.C.* Don Matejowsky, 7124 Jetty Ln., Houston, TX 77072

*Corpus Christi R.R.C.* John Polk, 1001 Louisiana, Corpus Christi, TX 78404

*Houston R.R.C.* J. Geller, 4132 Meyerwood, Houston TX 77025

*Texarkana R.R.C.* Bill Jones, 1209 Trinity, Texarkana, TX 77503

## UTAH

*Beehive T.C.* Jan Cheney, 289 South at 200 East, Kaysville, UT 84037

## VERMONT

*North Country A.C.* Robert Murphy, Rt. 3, Birchwood Park Dr., Barre, VT 05641

*Southern Vermont R.R.C.* Tom Wagner, 4 Caroline Dr., Bennington, VT 05201

*Vermont Ridgerunners* Tom Heffernan, Box 116, Killington, VT 05751

## VIRGINIA

*Rappahannock R.R.C.* Randall Washburn, 18 Heritage Rd., Fredericksburg, VA 22401

*Tidewater Striders* Robert Jennings, 1033 George Washington Highway W., Chesapeake, VA 23323

## WASHINGTON

*Bloomsday R.R.C.* Von Klohe, Box 645, Spokane, WA 99210

*Club Northwest* Bill Roe, 2557 25th Ave. E., Seattle, WA 98112

*Walla Walla Minimum Security R.R.C.* Louie Mendoza, Box 520, Walla Walla, WA 99362

*Walla Walla R.R.C.* Mack Bohlman, 1240 Boyer, Walla Walla, WA 99362

## WASHINGTON, D.C.

*D.C. Road Runners* David Gottlieb, 3115 Whispering Pines, Silver Spring, MD 20906

## WEST VIRGINIA

*Country Roaders R.R.C.* John Nally, 334 W. Cardinal Ave., Wheeling, WV 26003

*Kanawha Valley R.R.C.* Jim Jones, Box 2022, Charleston, WV 25327

## WISCONSIN

*Badgerland Striders* Clark Bowerman, 36545 Colonial Hills Dr., Dousman, WI 53118

*Indianhead T.C.* Bob St. Louis, 3352 Fear St., Eau Claire, WI 54701

## WYOMING

*Cheyenne T.C.* Brent Weigner, 421 E. 28th St., Cheyenne, WY 82001

*Human Energy West* Bruce Noble, 1063 Empanada, Laramie, WY 82071

# Age-Graded Scoring

Age affects performance. Times usually improve through a person's mid-twenties, level off for several years, then decline gradually. With this physical fact in mind, Ken Young of the National Running Data Center in Tucson generated scoring tables to correct for the handicaps of age. The following summary of his work. (So far, he has done this only for men's times.)

"Level I," 900 points, means runners can qualify for national-class competition in their particular age-groups. They can race the *equivalent* of a sub-4:10 mile or hold near-five-minute pace for a marathon. "Level II," 700 points, makes one a consistent leader in local events, capable of race times equal to a 4:30-4:40 mile or six-minute-paced marathoning. "Level III," 500 points, earns one respect as a committed racer with the ability to do an adjusted mile time of 5:15-5:30 and a marathon at a seven-minute pace.

Find your approximate point levels by interpolating for your age and time if they fall between the numbers listed.

| Event | | Age 10 | Age 20 | Age 30 | Age 40 | Age 50 | Age 60 | Age 70 |
|-------|-----|--------|--------|--------|--------|--------|--------|--------|
| **1500 m.** | I   | 4:32  | 3:45  | 3:48  | 4:05  | 4:30  | 5:00  | 5:33  |
|             | II  | 5:11  | 4:16  | 4:19  | 4:39  | 5:08  | 5:44  | 6:25  |
|             | III | 6:03  | 4:55  | 4:59  | 5:23  | 6:00  | 6:44  | 7:34  |
| **Mile**    | I   | 4:55  | 4:04  | 4:07  | 4:25  | 4:52  | 5:24  | 6:01  |
|             | II  | 5:38  | 4:37  | 4:40  | 5:02  | 5:34  | 6:13  | 6:56  |
|             | III | 6:35  | 5:20  | 5:24  | 5:50  | 6:30  | 7:18  | 8:12  |
| **2 miles** | I   | 10:55 | 8:46  | 8:45  | 9:21  | 10:18 | 12:28 | 12:46 |
|             | II  | 12:33 | 9:59  | 9:58  | 10:41 | 11:49 | 13:12 | 14:46 |
|             | III | 14:45 | 11:35 | 11:34 | 12:27 | 13:51 | 15:34 | 17:30 |

| | | | | | | | | |
|---|---|---|---|---|---|---|---|---|
| **5000 m.** | I | 18:00 | 14:09 | 14:00 | 14:53 | 16:22 | 18:14 | 20:20 |
| | II | 20:45 | 16:09 | 15:57 | 17:01 | 18:48 | 21:01 | 23:32 |
| | III | 24:28 | 18:47 | 18:32 | 19:51 | 22:03 | 24:48 | 27:55 |
| **6 miles** | I | 37:48 | 28:47 | 27:59 | 29:34 | 32:28 | 36:11 | 40:25 |
| | II | 43:41 | 32:54 | 31:57 | 33:50 | 37:19 | 41:45 | 46:49 |
| | III | 51:45 | 38:24 | 37:13 | 39:33 | 43:51 | 49:21 | 55:38 |
| **10 km.** | I | 39:18 | 29:53 | 29:02 | 30:40 | 33:40 | 37:31 | 41:55 |
| | II | 45:26 | 34:10 | 33:09 | 35:05 | 38:42 | 43:18 | 48:34 |
| | III | 53:50 | 39:52 | 38:37 | 41:01 | 45:29 | 51:11 | 57:42 |
| **15 km.** | I | 61:52 | 46:15 | 44:32 | 46:50 | 51:23 | 57:17 | 64:04 |
| | II | 71:38 | 52:57 | 50:53 | 53:38 | 59:06 | 66:09 | 74:16 |
| | III | 85:04 | 61:55 | 59:22 | 62:46 | 69:31 | 78:18 | 88:20 |
| **10 miles** | I | 66:55 | 49:53 | 47:58 | 50:25 | 55:19 | 61:41 | 68:59 |
| | II | 77:30 | 57:08 | 54:50 | 57:46 | 63:37 | 71:14 | 79:58 |
| | III | 92:04 | 66:50 | 63:59 | 67:36 | 74:52 | 84:18 | 95:04 |
| **20 km.** | I | 1:25 | 1:03 | 1:01 | 1:03 | 1:11 | 1:13 | 1:27 |
| | II | 1:39 | 1:12 | 1:09 | 1:13 | 1:20 | 1:25 | 1:41 |
| | III | 1:58 | 1:25 | 1:21 | 1:25 | 1:34 | 1:40 | 1:51 |
| **15 miles** | I | 1:45 | 1:17 | 1:14 | 1:17 | 1:25 | 1:35 | 1:46 |
| | II | 2:02 | 1:29 | 1:25 | 1:26 | 1:38 | 1:49 | 2:03 |
| | III | 2:25 | 1:44 | 1:39 | 1:40 | 1:55 | 2:10 | 2:26 |
| **25 km.** | I | 1:49 | 1:20 | 1:17 | 1:20 | 1:28 | 1:38 | 1:50 |
| | II | 2:07 | 1:32 | 1:28 | 1:32 | 1:41 | 1:54 | 2:08 |
| | III | 2:31 | 1:48 | 1:43 | 1:48 | 2:00 | 2:15 | 2:32 |
| **Marathon** | I | 3:15 | 2:22 | 2:15 | 2:21 | 2:35 | 2:53 | 3:14 |
| | II | 3:47 | 2:43 | 2:35 | 2:43 | 2:59 | 3:20 | 3:45 |
| | III | 4:31 | 3:12 | 3:02 | 3:11 | 3:31 | 3:58 | 4:29 |

# Purdy Scoring Tables

Computer scientist and running author Dr. J. Gerry Purdy of Denver devised the tables summarized here. They attempt to give equal weight to times at different distances. For instance, both a 4:00 mile and 2:17 marathon are worth 1000 points. Find your times on the chart. Most likely, they fall between 100-point levels. Estimate your true score, or figure exactly how many points you earn by using percentages of the listed times. For example: a mile of 4:25 is 63 percent better than the 500-point time, 37 percent below 600, so the score is 563. (Since greater numbers of women have run the longer races only in the last few years, Dr. Purdy's tables for women are not yet complete.)

## MEN'S EVENTS

| Event | 1000 | 900 | 800 | 700 | 600 | 500 | 400 | 300 | 200 | 100 |
|---|---|---|---|---|---|---|---|---|---|---|
| 1500 m. | 3:43 | 3:47 | 3:51 | 3:56 | 4:04 | 4:14 | 4:30 | 4:59 | 5:56 | 7:57 |
| Mile | 4:00 | 4:04 | 4:08 | 4:14 | 4:22 | 4:33 | 4:50 | 5:21 | 6:23 | 8:33 |
| 3000 m. | 7:55 | 8:04 | 8:12 | 8:26 | 8:42 | 9:08 | 9:50 | 11:05 | 13:23 | 17:29 |
| 2 miles | 8:31 | 8:40 | 8:50 | 9:04 | 9:22 | 9:50 | 10:35 | 11:56 | 14:24 | 18:48 |
| 3 miles | 13:12 | 13:26 | 13:43 | 14:05 | 14:35 | 15:21 | 16:37 | 18:50 | 22:40 | 29:09 |

| Event | 1000 | 900 | 800 | 700 | 600 | 500 | 400 | 300 | 200 | 100 |
|---|---|---|---|---|---|---|---|---|---|---|
| 5000 m. | 13:39 | 13:53 | 14:11 | 14:39 | 15:05 | 15:53 | 17:12 | 19:30 | 23:29 | 30:14 |
| 6 miles | 27:46 | 28:16 | 28:54 | 29:42 | 30:48 | 32:22 | 34:49 | 39:01 | 46:24 | 59:25 |
| 10 km. | 28:41 | 29:12 | 29:51 | 30:40 | 31:48 | 33:25 | 35:57 | 40:16 | 47:52 | 61:17 |
| 15 km. | 44:17 | 45:10 | 46:15 | 47:36 | 49:23 | 51:51 | 55:32 | 61:34 | 72:20 | 92:49 |
| 10 miles | 45:43 | 48:41 | 49:52 | 51:24 | 53:17 | 55:58 | 59:55 | 66:21 | 77:48 | 99:42 |
| 20 km. | 1:00 | 1:01 | 1:03 | 1:05 | 1:08 | 1:11 | 1:16 | 1:24 | 1:37 | 2:04 |
| 15 miles | 1:14 | 1:15 | 1:17 | 1:20 | 1:23 | 1:27 | 1:33 | 1:43 | 1:59 | 2:31 |
| 25 km. | 1:16 | 1:18 | 1:20 | 1:23 | 1:26 | 1:31 | 1:37 | 1:47 | 2:03 | 2:36 |
| 30 km. | 1:33 | 1:36 | 1:38 | 1:42 | 1:46 | 1:51 | 1:59 | 2:11 | 2:30 | 3:08 |
| 20 miles | 1:41 | 1:43 | 1:46 | 1:50 | 1:55 | 2:01 | 2:09 | 2:21 | 2:42 | 3:23 |
| Marathon | 2:17 | 2:20 | 2:25 | 2:30 | 2:37 | 2:45 | 2:56 | 3:12 | 3:38 | 4:28 |

## WOMEN'S EVENTS

| Event | 1000 | 900 | 800 | 700 | 600 | 500 | 400 | 300 | 200 | 100 |
|---|---|---|---|---|---|---|---|---|---|---|
| 1500 m. | 4:24 | 4:27 | 4:31 | 4:37 | 4:45 | 4:57 | 5:15 | 5:48 | 6:50 | 8:47 |
| Mile | 4:45 | 4:49 | 4:54 | 5:01 | 5:10 | 5:22 | 5:43 | 6:19 | 7:27 | 9:32 |
| 3000 m. | 9:40 | 9:47 | 10:02 | 10:18 | 10:39 | 11:08 | 12:00 | 13:24 | 15:42 | 19:23 |
| 2 miles | 10:24 | 10:32 | 10:47 | 11:04 | 11:27 | 12:00 | 12:54 | 14:24 | 16:53 | 20:51 |
| Marathon | 2:45 | 2:51 | 2:57 | 3:05 | 3:14 | 3:26 | 3:40 | 3:59 | 4:26 | — |

# Recommended Reading

**Beginner's Running Guide** by Hal Higdon. Everything a beginner needs to know to get started running on the right foot can be found in this book. The author draws on 30 years running experience to give you the most up to date and comprehensive knowledge in a breezy, personal style. Hardback $10.00.

**Dr. George Sheehan's Medical Advice for Runners** by Dr. George Sheehan. Here's Dr. Sheehan's first book designed to help you stay injury free. Dr. Sheehan feels that many running ailments are self-inflicted and therefore are preventable if we find and eliminate the cause. Hardback $10.95.

**The Complete Woman Runner** by the editors of *Runner's World*. Covering everything from getting started to entering competition once the body is properly conditioned, the book also contains a section on the mind and body of the woman runner: her potential and aptitudes. Hardback $10.95.

**The Complete Marathoner** edited by Joe Henderson. Written by top marathoners, this book offers advice for both the veteran and the first-time marathoner. There is emphasis on training, racing, and nutrition. Hardback, $10.95.

**Jog, Run, Race** by Joe Henderson. Leads the reader through several new beginnings—from walking to jogging, jogging to running, running to racing. Each beginning has a specific day by day progress guide. Paperback, $3.95.

**Long Run Solution** by Joe Henderson. Henderson devotes this book to the mental rewards of a sport whose popularity is now reaching mammoth proportions. More immediate than the physical benefits, the psychological effects of running are now being explored. Paperback, $3.95.

## Periodicals

**Runner's World**, America's leading running publication. Contains the most up-to-date information available on all aspects of running, including recreational, fitness and competitive running. 12 issues, $13 per year.

**Marathoner** is a high quality magazine you'll want to save: vibrant photographs, official coverage of major marathons and information on health and diet. Quarterly, $10 a year (4 issues) and $20 for two years (8 issues).

Available in fine bookstores and sport shops, or from:

## World Publications
Box 366, Mountain View, CA 94042

Include $.45 shipping and handling for each title (Maximum $2.25).